Praise for *Bunny*

"The twists and turns of this true-life story will keep you wanting to know more. It left me feeling a higher power was orchestrating Susan's journey."

—Kathleen Owen

"*Bunny* is a captivating story about an adopted daughter and her quest to find out about her biological family. Her perseverance was well worth what she discovered."

—Roberta Fife

"With a gentle style, author Susan Guillotte takes the reader through her quest to fill in the missing pieces of her ancestry. Not all the questions have answers and there are some surprises along the way."

—Brenda Foehrkolb

"*Bunny* is a story that sucks you in like undertow. I love it."

—Mary Lynn Landgraf

"One word came to mind: macramé. One knot at a time, weaving a story, a beautiful life."

—Michael Rydecki

"Thank goodness they chose life, or we would never have had you or this story."

—Dana Longest

Bunny

BASED ON A TRUE STORY

SUSAN D. GUILLOTTE

Text includes various name changes for privacy protection.

Dedicated to my "rocks"

Contents

PART ONE

Chicago, Illinois

CHAPTER ONE

"Wake up, Mama. It's time." It was a whisper with intention. The hallway light shone a line across her mother's sleeping body in the darkened bedroom. Betty shook her mother's shoulder gently, seeing the beginnings of awakening.

"I'm in labor. I called a cab." Her voice was soft and calm, trying to calm herself, as well. She knew well enough that the pain told her she had time, but it would still be unpredictable.

"Do you have your bag? Betty, are you okay? How bad are the pains?" Her mother came to full recognition of the moment, sitting up straight with the covers falling around her. Betty smiled at her mother's groggy recognition and felt her compassionate concern.

"I'm fine, not bad yet. I will call you if I can" she whispered as she leaned down to kiss her mother's forehead and then walked to get her coat and heavy scarf from the front room. She picked up the light bag and her pocketbook and turned out the light.

Betty left through the apartment door and headed for the lower lobby of the hotel apartment building. The big brass lobby clock showed the 2:00 a.m. hour her body already confirmed after lying awake for nearly two hours in her bed. Gus, the night auditor, was dozing in a nearly upright position and she walked quietly so as not to disturb him.

Betty saw the snow flurries drifting outside under the door lights and pulled her heavy coat collar tightly around her neck. Her waist area could not be protected from the bitter Chicago March wind. The waistband of the coat would never close over her pregnant stomach. As soon as she walked into the night air, the wind sliced at her face like a cold stinging whip. The waiting cab was a warm reward, but the smell of sauerkraut was almost as shocking as the wind had been.

"Where to, miss?" queried the back of a head with a tightly worn cap.

"Cook County Hospital . . . quickly please." That brought a quick glance into the driver's rear-view mirror. "I'll take you to the South Dorchester door unless you want another."

"No, that's fine."

The pains were coming a little faster. It was not like last time, slow and casual, but then the first time is always all new and like never again. Despite the icy patches and ice accumulation across the driver's windshield, the cabby made good time and pulled his cab as close to the hospital entrance as possible.

"Are you ok, miss?"

"I'm fine. Thank you. I can manage."

Betty paid the driver and gave the customary tip, grabbed her bag, and pushed herself out of the back seat. She found solid footing in her heeled pumps before stepping toward the hospital stairs, clutching tightly to the handrail for support and reassurance. The few steps were slippery, and she was slowly cautious.

The cab driver waited until she reached the top landing. Was there a hesitation at the door? Would he have to get out and help her through the front door entrance? A second later she reached for the large handle. She felt her left foot slide sideways when she grasped the heavy door to go inside.

Despite the hour of the night, it was warm and bright inside the hospital lobby. Betty moved toward the front desk where a matronly woman in a stiff white nurse's cap sat reading a book. Reaching the desk counter, Betty leaned quickly against the marble surface as a sharp pain climbed up her back and spasms pulled on both sides of her abdomen.

"May I help you, dear?" asked the nurse, as Betty's condition was hidden by the tall desk counter.

"I'm in labor," she answered simply.

"Oh, well let's get you taken care of!" the nurse responded, rising from her chair, and walking around the desk counter to Betty's side. "Come along this way," guiding her steadily down a long hallway.

CHAPTER TWO

After a brief examination, Betty was shown to a ward for women patients. There was a small nightstand for her belongings. The nurse from the front lobby passed her over to another nurse, a heavyset woman in her late forties who gave Betty a gown to wear and said she would be back in a few minutes.

Betty glanced around the large room. Half the beds were empty, and the others were occupied by sleeping women in the near-dark lighting. She stood behind the curtain and changed into the gown.

The bed was soft and clean. Already she would have loved to go to sleep but knew from experience that sleep would not be the case this morning. She unpacked her clothes and toiletries and placed all of them neatly in the nightstand drawer.

The nurse returned and checked Betty over medically for herself, determining that she was a healthy young woman with no additional medical issues with which to be concerned. She questioned the interval and severity of the labor pains. Betty told the nurse that she was working through The Cradle. The nurse smiled in response and said she would call them right away. The Cradle Society was a local organization that assisted any woman who wished to give up her baby for adoption.

An elderly doctor came in to see her next and asked more detailed questions about her pregnancy. He examined her physically and wrote notes on the papers. He said Dr. Phelps would be in the hospital soon and he would likely come in to see her straight away on his early rounds.

True to schedule, Dr. Phelps arrived within the next hour. He stopped methodically at all the other beds in the ward before seeing Betty last. He pulled the rollaway curtains around her bed and called for the day nurse to assist him in giving Betty a full examination. He reassured her that everything seemed normal. Dr. Phelps saw many young women like Betty. For a variety of reasons, she would not be keeping the baby. He was accustomed to the routine of steps required by The Cradle and would abide by their rules.

To put his own thoughts at rest, Dr. Phelps asked Betty the same questions he asked every woman in his care who had a plan such as hers. When the physical exam was over, the nurse removed the instruments and supplies and left the room. Dr. Phelps pulled up a chair from across the room and sat down next to her bed. He smiled at Betty and spoke quietly.

Dr. Phelps said, "Everything seems perfectly normal so far. Betty, are you quite certain you want to give up this baby?" She nodded slowly and said, "I am." Her face was blank and there were no tears. To his satisfaction, she seemed resolute. Sometimes the obvious question of *why* ran through his thoughts, but he never inquired out loud. He was fully aware of why many women made this decision. If she wanted to talk about it further, she would. Some women did but not Betty.

When it seemed certain she did not want to discuss more after that question, he asked her, "Do you want to see the baby before The Cradle takes it away?" He could see that she took a deep breath and shook her head, answering, "Doctor, I'm not sure." He understood. In his experience, that always seemed to be the harder question of the two and he would not pressure her to decide now.

Gradually the pains progressed as the normal, natural process played out. Betty did not cry or yell or complain. The nurses looked in on her and followed all medical procedures carefully. Time itself had its own schedule and the hours and many, many slow, pain-filled minutes culminated in the birth of a healthy baby girl twelve hours later.

Dr. Phelps was still at the hospital and helped Betty as best he could through the final birth moments. He assured her that everything was fine and patted her hand to commend her tireless, brave effort. He always admired the strength of women in this beautiful act of life, particularly, as he saw it, this completely unselfish, voluntary gift to the world. In his work, he saw many women who were unable to have children. If not for this loving act by Betty, they would never know the feeling of motherhood.

CHAPTER THREE

All the paperwork was in order when Mrs. Foley, the head nurse from The Cradle, arrived a short time after the birth. She read the notes silently to herself. The delivery was described as "easy and spontaneous."

The baby's arrival confirmed the expected pregnancy length of forty weeks. The baby girl weighed five pounds, twelve ounces, and her name was Cynthia. That was hospital policy. The maternity and pediatric staff picked a first name for the baby. It had to start with the first letter of the mother's last name. In most of the cases, The Cradle continued to use the name, as well.

Mrs. Foley complimented the hospital maternity ward nurse, Carla, on her excellent work. She was an experienced registered nurse and often handled The Cradle babies if time permitted, knowing very well how special rules applied to their cases.

"Nice work as always, Carla. Thank you. It makes our work so much easier. I'll check back tomorrow and the next day to follow up on the tests." Mrs. Foley picked up the baby in her arms, softly whispering, "Hello sweet Cynthia. You are a beautiful little girl." There were no tears from the baby. She placed her back gently in the bassinet on the far row of babies away from the viewing window. There would be no visitors for Cynthia other than Carla and Mrs. Foley.

"I'll go check on the mother. See you tomorrow, Carla."

Mrs. Foley knew her way around Cook County Hospital backwards and forwards. Most of her work centered inside the nursery halls and women's wards but occasionally the surgical staff was involved. It was always a delightful relief when the babies were healthy like Cynthia. She reached the women's area and walked the length of the long hallway to the ward furthest from the nurses' station. In the corner bed, she found

Betty, awake and resting comfortably.

"Hello, Betty," she spoke and smiled broadly. "No, don't sit up. How are you feeling? I am only here to make sure you are okay."

"I'm okay. My back still aches but I'm hoping that goes away soon."

"Betty, the baby girl is doing just fine. She seems very healthy, and all the signs appear well. Do you need anything? Can I get them to bring you something? Are you up to any dinner yet?" Betty smiled slightly at the report about the baby but asked for no other information. "No, I don't need anything more. The nurse said they would give me a very light snack and suggested I eat slowly. I do feel just a little bit hungry."

"Betty, I will be by every day to check on you. You did very well. Just rest as much as you can."

The next three days were filled with sleep and rest for Betty. There was only a small amount of pain and more discomfort than anything else. A pregnancy is hard on a human body, but Betty's overall good health and youth were strong components to a quick recovery.

The baby, Cynthia, continued to improve. The records showed a slight drop in birth weight on the first day but that could be expected. She passed all the tests, most importantly the Infant Kahn test for syphilis and the tuberculin test. She would be tested again and again.

As a healthy baby, Cynthia gradually increased her dietary intake like any normal baby. The record stated "Never breastfed" but the hospital nurses saw to it that Cynthia received a bottle feeding six times a day, every four hours. Three ounces disappeared on schedule every time.

On the third day, Mrs. Foley's visit would be different than her customary wellness check with good cheer. She entered Betty's ward and found her sleeping after a half-eaten breakfast tray had been pushed aside. Betty awoke when Mrs. Foley gently picked up a nearby chair to sit alongside her bed. Mrs. Foley carried a briefcase with her this morning and smiled warmly when she saw Betty's eyes open slowly.

"Good morning, Betty! How are you feeling this morning?" she queried softly.

"Much better Mrs. Foley. Much better than yesterday."

"I believe Dr. Phelps is going to release you today if you feel up to it. Do you think that will be okay? You might be very anxious to get out of here by now!" she added lightheartedly, opening her briefcase.

"I think that will be fine, Mrs. Foley. I can rest more at home" responded Betty.

"Betty, before you go home, we normally suggest that you sign the birth certificate and the final paperwork. As we told you last August when you came to us about the pregnancy, today's birth certificate will be sealed by the court, and no one will ever see it. A brand-new birth certificate will be created that does not identify you in any way. The new birth certificate will be created when we place the baby in a family, and the legal adoption will take place through the court. Do you think you feel up to signing the paperwork today?"

Betty nodded in agreement. She made her decision last August when she discovered that she was pregnant. There was legal recourse this day, but there was no argument in her heart. Betty knew that if she wanted to keep the baby, she could easily say so right now and there would be no retribution from The Cradle. Her circumstances were not good for keeping this baby and many reasons supported the adoption option. Still, in her heart, there was a tiny voice that urged her to shake her head slowly but unnoticeably. She pushed aside the tiny voice. She would go forward with her decision from last summer.

Mrs. Foley pulled out the Certificate of Birth first. In her experience, it was usually the hardest signature for mothers to sign. Although there indeed was a biological father somewhere, in the eyes of the Illinois state law, he had no claim to the child at all. His personal identification might be included in The Cradle's file but only for the sake of health and legally required information. Betty had supplied all she knew about the baby's father last August.

Betty straightened her position to sitting more upright in her bedcovers as Mrs. Foley handed her the clipboard holding the nearly blank form to sign. Few details would be completed until the lengthy legal process would progress. She did not read the completed or empty blanks as she signed on the bottom line.

Next, Mrs. Foley gave Betty the release form which gave The Cradle temporary custody of the baby. She explained, "Betty, this is the form that gives us temporary custody of the baby until the adoption can be finalized." Betty did not look up and did not speak as she accepted the form and signed her name where instructed.

"Well, Betty, that is all we need until we get in touch with you later in the process. Do you have any questions or concerns at all?" and she paused to let Betty think about anything she would like to say or ask.

"If you have any questions in the future, please call us or come and see us. If you have any problems with your health due to your pregnancy, please call us right away. We want to make sure you are okay." Betty nodded in understanding. "Take care, Betty" and Mrs. Foley rose to leave, replacing the chair in its previous location. She smiled at Betty and left the room.

Mrs. Foley walked directly toward the nursery and found Carla busy, tending to a bath for a newborn baby boy.

"Hi, Carla. I'm ready to take the baby Cynthia now. Are you free to sign the release?" Carla called to the nurse behind her to take over with the bath. "Sure, let's go."

Standing by the bassinet containing Cynthia, Carla checked over the baby's diaper and blanket for cleanliness, picked her up tenderly like a fragile, breakable object, and spoke softly to her, "Cynthia, you are on your way to a new life. God bless you, little one."

"Thank you, Carla. I'll see you again soon." Mrs. Foley took the baby in her arms and left the nursery. The private car and driver were waiting downstairs by the front entrance. Jackson, the driver, helped Mrs. Foley comfortably slide into the back seat of the car and they drove away slowly.

Back in the hospital women's ward, Dr. Phelps examined Betty for any signs that might indicate a problem after the baby's delivery. He questioned how she felt, and with all good results, he told her she could leave whenever she wanted. He urged her to not miss her follow-up appointments provided by The Cradle through the health clinic. He stressed how important it was for her health to make certain her body was healing well. He smiled supportively. She thanked him as he prepared to leave the ward.

Betty rose out of bed slowly, found her clothes in the small nightstand drawer, and changed out of her dressing gown. She slipped on her pumps and left the women's ward. Knowing it would still be freezing outside, she pulled her heavy coat gently but securely across the front of her body and walked down the long corridor. Downstairs, outside the front entrance, it was only seconds before she hailed a cab and asked the driver to take her home to the Harvard Hotel.

CHAPTER FOUR

After leaving outside the hospital entrance, Mrs. Foley asked Jackson to pull up directly to a private entrance in the back of The Cradle building. He carefully helped Mrs. Foley out of the car and carried her briefcase behind her. Inside, Mrs. Foley took the baby upstairs to the large nursery area. She was met by one of the head nurses who was instructed by Mrs. Foley to receive Cynthia. Then Mrs. Foley went downstairs to her office to register the new baby.

Mrs. Foley had been with the Cradle for twenty-seven years. It was created in 1923 by a woman who believed there was a need for an organization to help expectant mothers find a safe place for their babies. The organization would be a stalwart of professionalism and carry an impeccable reputation for excellence in care and recordkeeping. There could be no stain of backroom dealing, but a front room approach with compassion for the adults and loving dedication to the babies. The founder, Mrs. Walrath, held the strictest of standards for every activity and communication, and every employee and volunteer met those standards or was asked to leave.

Approaching her office, Mrs. Foley saw a young couple entering Mrs. Walrath's office down the hall. There were many reasons why young couples could not have children and often they would come to The Cradle as a last resort. Mrs. Walrath would interview them and explain the procedures of adoption, and it was always a shock for them to learn that the process could possibly take as long as five years to receive a baby. During that period of time, it was suggested that the prospective mother volunteer her time in the nursery. Most women were eager to participate in the program and quickly signed up for the next scheduled training class. The Cradle never charged a fee for adoption, relying on donations, so volunteers were a valuable part of the organization.

Mrs. Foley sat at her office desk and began the organization of Cynthia's records. She rechecked the list of tests performed by the hospital staff and doctors. More tests would be in order over the next few weeks and months at The Cradle. So far, Cynthia was a healthy, growing baby entrusted into their care. She would be monitored twenty-four hours a day, seven days a week, recording every detail of her early beginning. The head nurse began a chart for Cynthia in the nursery. It would be checked and rechecked constantly to ensure no facts were missed, and no signs unseen.

Her work complete, Mrs. Foley rose to get her coat and leave for the day. Out the single window in her office, a large black limousine caught her eye as it approached the back private entrance. She paused out of curiosity and watched a driver get out of the vehicle, move to the opposite side, and open the back door.

A large man climbed out of the back seat and leaned his two arms back into the car. A young woman held what appeared to be a baby in her arm, and the large man helped her out. They disappeared inside the back entrance to The Cradle. It was a scene Mrs. Foley had seen more than a few times over her twenty-seven years with the organization. All the parents, and indeed the babies, arrived through The Cradle's doors in a variety of ways and circumstances.

PART TWO

South Haven, Michigan

CHAPTER FIVE

He was an odd boy, even back then, and he fit the typical image of the only child that many parents fear their first child will become—introverted and somewhat unapproachable. Was he born that way, or did they inadvertently or unknowingly mold him into something they did not particularly care for?

Perhaps the term "care for" was a bit cold in regard to parenting. Most days, his father just did not have any idea what to do with him. For whatever reason, Don Dickinson was the couple's only child and would remain that way. Like most children of the early 1930s, Don was rarely home, and most parents had enough to worry about without dwelling on their ordinary or even not-so-ordinary boy's activities.

Introverted was an understatement for Don. When he was at home, he spent all his time in his attic bedroom reading any books he could find. His father worked long hours at the phone company, a self-made man having very little education, but who had trained himself in the ways of the world by reading every volume of the Encyclopedia Britannica in the local library. His mother did what mothers do and young boys usually never notice—caring for the home and family members' needs.

They were a wealthy family in comparison to the dismal standards of many other families hit painfully hard by the Depression, but not wealthy enough to be free of worry and shortages. If Don ever lived beyond a mashed potato for dinner nearly every night, he swore to himself he would never eat another.

Don was in Miss May's fourth-grade class at Central School. By the fourth grade, many of the teachers know for sure who has exceptional skills and who doesn't. Miss May could see a future in Don. He was too busy being a boy to think about the future, but he easily took his studies seriously. An A grade could have stood for "Automatic."

* * *

Normally, he looked forward to getting out of class and joining up with his best pal, Eugene. Today he dreaded the thought.

Don got a big shiny new bicycle for Christmas. In Eugene's eyes, Don's parents were definitely rich, and everyone knew it. Don's father worked for the Union Telephone Company and of course, they had a telephone—a measurement of wealth in the small town and something other people could easily live without. Despite years of use, the telephone still remained a mystery to many people. The mystery was how it worked. If heaven was based on 99% faith, then the telephone system was a close 98%. In 1934, that mystery and its use was simply not a priority for many people.

Since Christmas, Don had avoided the bicycle. He had not wanted it. Some of the boys had bikes but if Eugene did not have one, what good would it be for Don to have it? Don had no idea how to ride it and there was more trouble with his dilemma: he was afraid of heights. Not a tree climber by choice, he was even uncomfortable looking out his third-floor attic bedroom window. The bicycle seat did not really look very high, but it had the appearance that it would *feel* terribly high, just as bad.

There was also his pride to consider, what little he had. He was self-conscious enough with the skinny build and thick glasses. His physical features contributed to his one good comedy impression, that of Stan Laurel. Don practiced imitating the celebrity's voice and mannerisms often, but the rest of the created image was all natural.

Embarrassment in attempting to conquer the monster of public bicycle riding would seal his fate as a complete fool in the first ten feet of effort. Although his father had never mentioned the gift after Christmas day, Don could not keep it hidden forever. It was late spring now.

"Ya gotta help me," he begged Eugene, and Eugene would play him along as usual. "Look Don, you just gotta get on it and tame her. Who hasn't learned to ride yet? Only you." He cut his eyes at Don and added, "It's too cold today but tomorrow is the day. We'll go down to Sunset Drive. There's only one house on that street." He knew Don was scared to death that someone would see him.

Eugene was the middle brother of the three oldest children in the Wheeler family. He was the darling, the best looking, and he had the whole world of South Haven charmed. In his young eyes, he thought of the whole town as his friend, but Don was something different. Perhaps he felt sorry for Don in his heart without even realizing it, but the end result was a solid affection between the boys that approached a feeling of family brotherhood. Their relationship would not eliminate teasing one another but there was always a soft safety net nearby.

Joe was the oldest Wheeler brother to Eugene and the smartest. After Eugene, came Evert, the baby. By today's standards, the three of them could have been considered a street gang but it was a different time back then. Their mother had a house to clean and laundry and meals for seven and a brand-new baby. Their father worked for the post office and volunteered for the fire department when he wasn't doing his favorite pastime of fishing, if only to have the peace and quiet. If the kids were not in school, they were given sandwiches in the morning and told not to come home until supper. Their mother usually packed one for Don as well.

CHAPTER SIX

Like everything in South Haven, activities were predetermined by the weather. The best time was always summer at the lake. There were swimming and climbing races out to the lighthouse, and sailing if you were lucky enough to have a boat or know someone who did. Lake Michigan was dear to their hearts, but it could be an unforgivingly vicious foe when a storm appeared out of nowhere.

Of course, with Joe being the older brother, he always seemed to have the best ideas. The previous August, the boys set up a camp in a quiet section of beach by the lake. Joe decided they would all be pirates, serious pirates, that day. Pirate adventures could be great fun.

There was always a good supply of wood along that south end of the beach, courtesy of storms. That particular crescent-shaped area of South Haven's shoreline collected a big enough inventory to complete their camp area and the ship-building plans. After a few days of diligent collecting of materials, they tied the extra logs and boards together to make a raft.

"We need to test it to make sure our pirate ship will float," concluded Don. Of course, he was more interested in building the ship than sailing it because he had no idea how to swim, probably the only boy in South Haven who never learned, yet another factor which he was sure somehow reduced his application to a state of full manhood.

Joe assumed the leadership role and pushed the raft-like vessel into the gentle waves, out to a depth of about two feet of the bitterly cold lake water. The boys watched solemnly from the beach. Joe climbed aboard and the raft submerged about two inches under his meager weight, but it did not sink to the bottom. He raised his fists in the air like a winning prizefighter and the boys cheered from the beach. They all waded into the water to get a triumphant Joe and raft back to the beach. It was a glorious day for the pirate group.

After a long day of pirate work, the Wheeler boys and Don went home, always looking forward to dinner. Joe and Eugene sat at the table in their places along with their sisters, Delores, and tiny baby LaVerta. Their father sat at one end of the table and everyone waited for their mother to sit down as well.

"Where is Evert? Go get him, Joe" asked their mother of her oldest son.

Joe looked at Eugene inquiringly. Apparently, Joe needed to inform his parents of their important work that day. "Evert is a pirate now, a real one," he answered proudly. Eugene nodded in impressed approval.

Since Evert was the youngest and the lightest of the group, they had tied Evert to the raft for safety so he would not fall off and pushed him out into the lake on an important pirate mission to return with many treasures.

"What??????" their mother shrieked in horror and fell slowly into her chair. "Joe, you go down there right now and get him back. Joseph—" she spoke to their father, "—you don't come back either without Eve." She would not cry until they left the house. They returned in one hour. Evert had floated right back to the beach with the waves, but he was happy to see his brothers and have help getting the wet knots untied.

After dinner that night, all their mother would say to their father was, "Joe, you need to have a talk with those boys," and so they went fishing the next morning. Enough would be said then. But, regardless of the many talks their father gave them, there was always something in the works with those Wheeler boys.

Their sister Delores was a year younger than Evert and rarely would a toy last a whole year for her. When she got a dollhouse for Christmas, the boys got a fire engine. The dollhouse served as a perfect building to set on fire in the backyard so they could use their fire engine. When she got a doll baby for Christmas, the boys got a doctor kit, and operated on all parts of the doll, but unfortunately could not save its life. With three older brothers, Delores had to get tough.

Eventually, Eugene helped Don master the bicycle on Sunset Drive.

They were pretty sure no one saw the wobbling wheels and shaking legs or heard the rising, pitched voice. Only a few scuffs later and Don was moving along at a good clip. It wasn't so bad. At least it would make a quick trip to the library on Phoenix Street.

All was fine with the bicycle until one trip on his way home from the library and a book started to slip through his arm. He did not see the truck parked in front of a house around the next corner. When he looked up at the last second, he swerved the front wheel to avoid the back of the truck and ran the front wheel up a tree, crashing it into a broken pile. Don walked the broken bicycle home. His father took it away and he never saw it again.

CHAPTER SEVEN

Summers in South Haven carried many other activities. For one example, the band practice never stopped. Every child was in some form of band or orchestra, thanks to the interminable dedication of Mr. Listiak, the music teacher.

Every child began to learn an instrument at a young age. Mysteriously, it often seemed to be related to their teeth. If their teeth were bucked, they started on the trumpet. If they had a split in their front teeth, they started on the flute. Whatever they were given, they played with no question unless its use was totally intolerable to those listening nearby. Instruments were passed around like used clothing and band uniforms especially survived years of wear. Talented hands were constantly mending and tailoring as needed, never wasting.

Besides the band practice and marching hours over the short Michigan summer months, there was plenty of time for swimming in the lake, playing on the beaches, and climbing trees. Children were rarely inside unless a storm was so bad that it disrupted a game completely.

There was a constant flow of wealthy tourist travelers into the small town. Hundreds came across the lake on large steamer ferries from Wisconsin or up from Chicago. A variety of resorts welcomed the visitors, creating a multitude of simple summer jobs for any enterprising youngsters.

Bag boys, kitchen help, and extra shop worker positions provided money for families who still suffered under the remnants of the Great Depression. When the school year approached, some of the resorts closed for the winter, and that coincided with the end of their employment—and the need to once again prioritize their studies.

In the Wheeler household, there was always music. If the children weren't practicing their instruments, they were singing constantly. Joe was the oldest and starting the fifth grade, Eugene was next in the fourth grade, and Evert was the youngest boy, climbing into third grade.

Delores, the first girl in the family, had the best voice of the group and it gave her a solid hold of respect in her position with her older brothers. At an early age, she began to sing for funerals and weddings, earning a small reward which she cleverly turned into candy purchases that she shared with them.

Don loved to sing with them also although his voice was definitely the weakest of the group. No one cared; they just sang. Although he was younger than Eugene, the teachers pushed him through the lower grades over a period of months and he arrived two years ahead, landing in Eugene's class, cementing their friendship even more. The first day of school was exciting and they all soon settled into study routines.

Delores was not an exceptional student, but she held her own compared to the other girls in her second-grade class. It did not help that she crossed arms with her teacher, Miss Greef. With a name like that, it would be hard to expect otherwise.

Miss Greef had a frightful reputation for her dealings with any unruliness from her students. She took it upon herself to instill manners and good study habits into all her students at an early age. When it came time to enforce this theory on Delores, Miss Greef was aware of the challenge upon her, having been terrorized annually by Delores's three older brothers in prior years. As the preacher liked to say, it came to pass, and frightfully.

Over the summer months, Delores was old enough to begin learning new skills. Her mother taught her to sew by hand and she took to it right away, darning every sock she could get her hands on. She hunted through piles of clean laundry for any necessary mending that caught her eye.

She talked the dressmakers in town into saving their tiniest scraps for Delores and she savored making tiny doll clothes by hand. This little project did not stop in her school year. When Miss Greef caught Delores's hand sewing during the study hour, she promptly took it out of her hands and disciplined her hands with a ruler.

Delores also began to learn baton twirling over the summer. It almost became an obsession, practicing outside on sun-filled days and inside on rainy ones. She learned all the moves her neighbor friend's older sister could think of to show her, so she invented many new ones on her own. After Miss Greef left the room to take a sick child to the principal's office one day, Delores took the opportunity for more practice until the baton flew out of Delores's hand and broke a window. It was going to be a long year for Delores and would feel even longer for Miss Greef.

During the first month of school, parts were handed out for the upcoming Christmas play so that lines could be memorized, and costumes and sets could be prepared. It was a busy time for Delores, angel duty in the play with soloist and chorus parts combined. Her brothers were shepherds again, but Don's thick glasses relegated him to the chorus completely. He could not go without them and walk a straight line safely.

It was the Christmas play that cemented Delores's one-sided love affair with Don. There was just something about him in that chorus that she had sensed before but now knew was solidly in her heart. Don needed someone and it might as well be her. He had Eugene to share boy stuff but someone else would just have to teach him a lot of everything else that he was no doubt lacking, being a boy, after all. She would be that person.

Delores would stare at the back of his head when the classes lined up for dismissal from school. Sometimes he would turn around and search the faces as if sniffing out each person's eyes to find the stare that was prickling his back neckline; his eyes resting confidently on Delores's face, knowing it could not be her.

CHAPTER EIGHT

Over the next ten years, there were many changes to affect the children's young lives in their small town. Another family member joined the Wheeler house: their grandmother came to live with them, staying mostly inside the house. She had lost her leg, a story that remained truly incomprehensible to the children, and she was grouchy and unhappy most of the time in her wheelchair. They would creep around her trying to not be seen. She did not even sing.

High school brought more activities, the band being the most prominent. The boys played basketball for fun, but band practice was like work. Mr. Listiak required musical practice almost daily and Mr. Ames designed the formations and practice routines. They wondered if he stayed up all night dreaming of diabolical combinations of marching patterns.

Most days required field practice, with and without instruments, including a few rainy days. They had to learn to ignore the rain and cold, and march onward. Every person followed the person in front of them and the drum major's whistle and baton. Most of the kids in South Haven walked wherever they went and the constant marching no doubt gave them all the strongest leg muscles east of the Mississippi River.

Joe Wheeler was the drum major for three years of high school. He was the tallest boy, and his top hat made him into a marching tower. Eugene and Evert played horns and Delores was a majorette. She practiced baton incessantly with her best friends and cousin. The hard work paid off when she became a drum majorette with her brother.

Aside from band practice, Delores was very active with her singing voice. High school gave her four years of Glee Club, Acapella Choir, Girl's Trio, band, baton, and dance. Her voice became her dominant strength, after trying substitute teacher and librarian assistant activities unsuccessfully.

Delores's mother had been Miss South Haven in her youth. Delores's beauty, beaming smile, and personality won her many boys' attention and several girl pals but the snagging of Don would require some brotherly assistance by Eugene.

"I'm telling you, Don, she's a sure bet. She's crazy about you. You can't lose," Eugene advised him this morning.

"If you're setting me up, Gene, I'm coming after you."

It had been a few tough years for Don. His father divorced his mother and she moved away to the nearby town of Grand Rapids, rarely seeing Don much afterward. The divorce was only explained as "something between adults." Rather than approaching his father's quiet distance, he had always been closer to his mother.

Although Don could never consciously define it by himself, in his heart, his mother had been the only loving spirit in the household. After she left, his father's parents came to live with them, and Don's grandmother took up his mother's homemaking. He spent even more time on his studies or reading alone. Don did not participate in band activities. His father still insisted that he study violin, so for his high school years, he was active in the school orchestra. He never achieved first chair position which was a quiet relief to him.

Finally, under Eugene's solemn advice, in his second year of high school, Don acquired the courage to ask Delores to the picture show, knowing he could go after Eugene if it all went bust. Don worked at The Michigan Theatre on Saturday evenings, and he would not need to get tickets for them to see the show, but he would spend the money for a soda and a Moon Pie. She would like that. The theatre was the only place in town to get them. The owner brought them up from Tennessee.

That first movie show began a friendship that Delores had waited years on which to embark. She was finally achieving her first step towards marrying Don Dickinson. He did not ask her to date only him, so she continued to be sought after by several other boys in high school.

"I told you she would go out with you! When are you going to learn that I know what is best for your love life?" laughed Eugene. He was dating two girls this weekend. "In spite of the fact she is my sister, she's still about the most popular girl in the school. You know she was talking to Jack Collier. He told me he thinks she is the most."

"Well, I can't marry her, Gene. I can't even watch her every minute. What else can I do?"

"For one thing, you need to join the band. There is an open spot in the cymbals section since Harry Wake got sick again."

"You know my father won't let me quit the orchestra."

"You don't have to. Any nut can play the cymbals and you'll be able to ride the bus to football games and keep an eye on her." Eugene saw a glimmer of interest on Don's face.

So, Don spoke with Mr. Ames, and he agreed to let Don start out as a cymbals player but warned him that if Harry came back, he would have to give his slot back to Harry. Harry never did, moving instead to Chicago to live with his aunt to be closer to the hospital there.

CHAPTER NINE

The faraway rumblings of war in Europe were a distant hum in their young lives. Parents who had fought in the big war that "would end all wars" raised little interest in going back to fight someone else's trouble, and their lives were just starting to climb out of the economic misery of the 1920s and 1930s.

The town of South Haven had now developed into a choice vacation destination for the many wealthy travelers coming across Lake Michigan from Chicago and Minneapolis. Steamers now brought them by the thousands, weekend after weekend for a two dollar roundtrip passage. South Haven was growing in many directions due to all the tourist money.

Aside from helping the existing industries, the lumber companies could not supply new lumber fast enough to meet growth demands. New businesses of all types, such as a photography studio, a yacht club on the Black River, as well as bakeries and grocery stores blossomed like spring flowers, and many families thrived. One of the largest covered dance floors in the country was a great attraction with name bands visiting often. There was a large variety of lodging resorts of all designs, themes, and interests.

After his high school graduation, Joe went off to college in Cleveland. He came home to South Haven and worked through his summer vacations. Thanks to the continuing increase in tourists, there were lots of summer jobs for youngsters and the boys stayed busy. Delores continued to sing at weddings and funerals, counted bugs in the fields for the local chemical company, and worked as a lifeguard on the lake, once helping to save seven sailors off a capsized vessel.

In addition to his theatre job, Don was hired on to help crew the local sailing sloops called Lightnings, popular sailboats on Lake Michigan. There was a rumor that their small but growing town of South Haven might host the North American Lightning Class Sailing Championships in a year or two and he hoped to be a part of it.

The news of the attack on Pearl Harbor came as a shock to everyone. Of course, there was talk beforehand that the fighting in Europe could escalate, but most people were not eager to send their children to do what they had done already. The boys, however, had a different outlook. Joe registered for the draft in February 1942 and then joined the US Navy. He stayed in the Navy for many years and went back to college to become a dentist after the war.

Eugene agreed to his parents' request to wait until after graduation in June and joined the Marines. He was assigned to the 1st Raider Battalion, D Company. He would not be as fortunate as his brothers, dying bravely in a bloody, poorly directed battle on New Georgia Island among the group of Solomon Islands in the Pacific campaign.

Eugene died on July 5, 1943. Like many families throughout the war, the Gold Star Family designation was an honor but a bitter consolation. The news of the poor strategy by Eugene's battle commander added a layer of tragedy to the loss of lives so far away. Like most people, family members wore the traditional black armbands for a year in respect for their loved one. Eventually and sadly so, that tradition would disappear in American life. It had a wonderful purpose in a community, reminding other people they met to be compassionate with them in their grief.

Evert and Don, being the same age, registered for the draft in 1942 but Evert did not join the Marines until after his 1943 high school graduation. He became a tank driver. Later they would refer to the tanks as "creeping coffins." He survived the duration of the war in Europe but when he came home, he never seemed the same. He spent a lot of time at home with his mother and dad unlike many young men returning from war. It took a long time to settle on a wife and get married, but he lived happily after that.

Don had already graduated from high school, registering for the draft in that June of 1942, but the Army would not take him. He could not see without his thick glasses, he had completely flat feet and was totally color-blind. Instead, they used him often to help with camouflage testing and development.

The military would take him up in a plane and fly over different areas to see if his eyes could see the camouflage tents or vehicles. Colors all stood out differently to color-blind people. If his eyes could not see the patterns, then that was the best camouflage they could design. Except for participating in those tests, the army told him to go to college as he had planned.

Don felt privately that he was simply rejected by the military, and never felt like he contributed to the war as other men did. He was devastated by Eugene's death as if he had lost a brother. He thought for certain that he would never have that kind of friendship again.

PART THREE

*Evanston, Illinois and then
Arlington Heights, Illinois*

CHAPTER TEN

Northwestern University opened up a brand-new world for Don and he became a brand-new person in it. It was located about three hours from South Haven in a suburb of Chicago. His father could not afford all the costs of college but helped with the majority. Upon arrival at the campus, Don checked the advertisements for a job. One ad offered room and board, just what he needed, including a very small salary as well. It listed an address, and he walked there straight away.

The house on Barron Street was massive in size. An aging butler answered the ringing doorbell and inquired about the purpose of Don's call. The gentleman showed him to the small office in the rear of the first floor so filled with books that it could hardly house one more. Something wonderful smelled from a nearby kitchen and Don closed his eyes to soak in the scents, as if a smell could be some form of nourishment.

The room was darkly furnished but a warm breath of light shone through a row of gigantic windows behind the desk. It framed a beautiful garden scene of roses and late summer flowers. Two large statues stood in the center of the lawn. Don politely did not sit but chose to stand while he waited for the man of the house to appear.

The man was not a man at all but a stately woman, perhaps sixty years old. Her name was Mrs. Ewen and she inquired as to Don's "full name" as she referred to it. She motioned with her hand and suggested that he sit in one of the large armchairs in front of the carved desk.

She sat down slowly behind the desk and began to discuss the business at hand. Mrs. Ewen explained that she was a widow and lived alone. What she needed was a butler, as the aging gentleman who answered the door could no longer climb the extensive stairs throughout the home. He was going to live with his sister in Indiana as soon as a replacement could be found.

Don did not speak. Mrs. Ewen sat stiffly behind the heavy desk, directing him to provide his background information and explain to her what lead him to apply for the position. "What are your credentials? Whom have you worked for before?"

"Mrs. Ewen, I have never been a butler. In fact, I have never seen one until today." He looked at the high walls of books surrounding Mrs. Ewen's desk as his eyes circled around the room. "But I can learn." He told her that he was enrolled as a freshman at Northwestern.

Mrs. Ewen studied him seriously, no doubt with genuine concern for his youth and lack of any experience or culture. "Where are you staying?" she inquired.

"I have a temporary room, but I will need to find less expensive arrangements." She studied his well-kept appearance and manner of composure and speaking. She knew that Gibbs was anxious to retire and relax a bit.

"You may have the position. Gibbs will not be leaving for a few days so that he can have ample opportunity to show you what I need. When he leaves, you may have his room in the attic, your meals in the kitchen as cook allows, and Sundays off. I will provide you two suit uniforms that must be washed out daily by you so that every day has a clean suit. I will expect you to be here unless you have class or school requirements on a minimum basis. Are you agreeable to that?"

The room, the books, and the intoxicating smell of some kind of unnamable meat were perhaps almost overwhelming to a young man who had not eaten since his father placed him on the train to come to Evanston about midmorning. He could not say yes fast enough. He would continue to rent his lodging until it was time for Mr. Gibbs to leave for Indiana.

Indeed, Don learned how to "buttle" quickly from Mr. Gibbs, who had been working for the Ewen family for over thirty years. He was a kind and friendly fellow and Don wished he were not leaving. It would be Don's duty to maintain the callers and see to Mrs. Ewen's needs when she entertained, which occurred more frequently than Don would have guessed.

Mrs. Ewen was very active in her community and socially speaking, she was extremely well liked. Her spirit of generous charity exposed a very giving and compassionate heart and Don began to admire her very much. It was almost motherly when she tried to plan her home entertaining around Don's class schedule. In return, he never failed to be a good house guest and employee.

The other house employees were friendly enough and welcomed Don by simply leaving him alone. There was a gardener who also helped inside the house with repairs or any heavy jobs that required two men's muscles. He was always outside soon after dawn, maintaining the beautiful gardens, lawns, and walkways. Clearing the snow was his solitary winter activity and the lake effect provided its continual bounty of snowfall.

The cook accepted him distantly at first. No doubt she wondered about how much a young college boy would want to eat. Mr. Gibbs had been so predictable in timing and quantity. But Don seemed happy with any leftover foods that cook had on hand and, conveniently, he would take them any time she was ready to get them out of her kitchen. He was also helpful with the washing up if he had time. From Don's perspective, he had never seen such wonderful food, and he experienced new things he had never even heard of. He was so grateful for his position.

CHAPTER ELEVEN

Don continued through his first two years of college, going home to South Haven for Eugene's funeral when the military shipped his body home. In most cases, surviving spouses or parents were allowed to choose a burial site for their loved ones. It could be near the battle where he lost his life with many other soldiers, or he could be brought home. In Eugene's case, his mother could not imagine leaving him in a foreign land and the family waited patiently at the station until the train arrived on the given day.

Don felt devastated by Eugene's death all over again, not only because he knew how painful it would be for everyone, but because Eugene had been like no one else in his life. There was a trust there, a comfort he could never begin to see in other male acquaintances, even his fraternity brothers. He knew the value of all friends but there was something different about Eugene.

Don and Delores still dated when he visited South Haven. He would write to her and let her know that he would be coming home. Don went home for Christmas, and a month in summer was generously provided by Mrs. Ewen when she went on holiday herself. He had no expectations of exclusivity with Delores, and she was still one of the most popular girls in the school. She graduated from high school on June 6, 1944, and wrote to him that she would be attending Northwestern in the fall. Her parents had saved enough money to pay most of her school costs.

When Delores arrived at Northwestern by train to begin her college life, Don felt obligated to meet her there. He helped her to the women's dorm, stealing a kiss along the way. She had literally blossomed into much more of a beauty than he even remembered. It was unclear how she could look so different here in Evanston than she had looked in South

Haven. In addition, Don noticed right away that there were admiring glances from many classmates outside her dormitory entrance.

Delores jumped into her music education classes with full force and still worked continually on her voice training. Her music degree required that she learn to play some type of song on every instrument in the orchestra. Over the years, she accomplished respectable verses on most of them except the tuba. Three Blind Mice was her best performance on that dreadful thing, but she passed the class with a good grade.

One of her other challenges was learning Italian. She could sing it any time, but memorizing all the verb conjugations was tedious to the point of putting her to sleep in the late-night study hours. Thankfully her sorority sister coached her in detail and especially the pronunciations. Perhaps if she just sang her way through all the tenses, it might accomplish a passing grade.

Don's education was much more ethereal in his studies of psychology. He analyzed human behavior and would often comment on her actions in comparison to the latest professor's lecture, something she tolerated patiently and laughed away. Sometimes it baffled Don as to how the lecture by the professor made such perfect sense until he tried to apply the same thoughts toward Delores' behavior. For some reason, it was never totally predictable.

As in high school, Don wanted to test his debate club skills on those around him but found very few takers who could match him. In Delores' opinion, he was doing too much thinking and not enough dancing. His grades were perfect and she could not fault him for that. He won so many awards and competitions that she could not remember half of them. He finally decided to join a fraternity in his sophomore year and early in her first quarter of college, he offered her his pin. She accepted, happily.

* * *

Don graduated from college in 1946 with the highest honors, including Phi Beta Kappa. He wanted to become an executive, maybe oversee huge companies. His first job was in a Chicago bobby pin factory working in the personnel office, but he had to spend a lot of time filling in for the man who stirred the vat of liquid used to coat the bobby pins. It was a job and it did not pay very much. With the war finally over, jobs were beginning to be scarce, so he stayed far longer than he hoped. He had to pay his bills, sharing an apartment with three other fraternity brothers.

Delores graduated in 1948 and planned to teach music if she could find an open position. What she really had planned was to marry Don Dickinson but all their talk about it just seemed to only procrastinate the plan. In fact, there was really no plan at all.

Delores would have to make a choice and, as she saw it, so would he. Under some degree of duress, he agreed to get married. *Would he ever be ready*, he wondered, and the truthful answer was probably not. The reality was that he could not find a more perfect wife, beautiful, educated, talented, and fun, and to complete his ideal future, he was pretty sure that every man needed a wife.

Delores wired her parents and they came to Evanston on the train to witness the simple ceremony. They brought their youngest child, Delores' youngest sister, Diane, who was only three years old. It was an exciting trip for her mom and dad to come to the big city.

While Delores' parents got to do a little sightseeing around Chicago, Don and Delores took Diane down to the Cook County clerk's office and placed Diane on the long office counter, announcing that they needed a marriage license. Assuming Diane was their child, the clerk was appalled when they both said it was their first marriage, and disapprovingly glared at the three of them. "I guess you certainly *do* need a license!" she snapped.

CHAPTER TWELVE

The newlyweds had no honeymoon. There was no extra money for a luxury like that. Don needed to find a better job and took a very junior position in the personnel department of a local plumbing manufacturing company. Delores treated herself to a name change, choosing to shorten Delores to Dee but always referring to herself as Mrs. Donald Dickinson first. She liked the ring of Dee Dickinson and indeed, it fit her personality perfectly.

They set up their new living arrangements in a basement apartment in Evanston. It was cramped and damp, but they hardly noticed. It was moderately furnished but Dee was industrious. She had taken sewing in college and had a used black porcelain Singer featherweight sewing machine. Given any amount of fabric and that machine, she hoped to work miracles. She gave away the dismal curtains and made ruffled new ones with a spark of color and gaiety, completely changing the atmosphere in their two rooms. It was amazing what a little color could do, she thought.

Dee was offered a position at Swarthmore School as a music teacher. It was exactly what her degree in Music Education had trained her to do, and she worked hard to help her students appreciate and play music in a variety of ways. She was even able to utilize her minor from college, which was Voice, singing with her students as much as possible. It warmed her heart to have even the toughest student respond well. She laughingly told Don that it was tough to be a tough guy when they were singing.

Through a friend's connection, she began to do some modeling through a local finishing school. To her surprise, she earned more money in half the time than she did as a music teacher. She was so successful at modeling that the owner asked her to join their school as a director and as a teacher. It was not an easy decision, loving both places of employment, but she decided in the end to resign from Swarthmore at the end of the school year.

Dee found that she really enjoyed working with all the young women students at the school. They were enrolled in the school for many different reasons. Some women simply wanted to learn manners, grace, and poise. The culture of the time gave great value to refinement and elegance. The ladies studied walking, sitting, communications, speech, and even dining etiquette.

Most of the young women studied very hard and it was wonderful to watch them usually develop their own style, deportment, quality of fashion, and image. Many women were about to start their life's careers and just wanted to feel polished and confident in any situation. If they could not learn those things at home, the school gave them a safe and supportive environment.

The father of her close friend, Kaye, came to see her one day and asked if she would be interested in starting a modeling school of her own with his daughter if he would fund their startup costs. She and Kaye began the North Shore Models' Finishing School in March 1950, on Davis Street, offering small classes and individual attention for modeling trainees and career girls. They also trained beauty pageant contestants. It was certainly a thrill to see one of their students receive the coveted title of Miss Illinois.

THE EVANSTON REVIEW   *March 30, 1950*

KAYE   and DEE DICKINSON

announce the opening of

The North Shore Models' Finishing School

with offices and studios located in the
heart of Evanston at 605 Davis Street

Telephone: GReenleaf 5-2840

Small classes and individual attention for
modeling trainees, career girls, high school
and college students, and children.

Spring classes now forming.

Don came home one evening to find Dee busily preparing dinner in their tiny kitchen. There were tears on her cheeks and falling to the sink basin below. Dee would not look at him. He gently grasped her arms and turned her slightly to face him.

"What in the world has happened? Are you ok?" he asked, slightly panicked by her tears, his mind racing to what she could have encountered in her normal busy day with the modeling school—or maybe someone had died? She dropped the utensils in the sink and tried to raise the courage to tell him what was wrong.

"I went to the doctor this afternoon because I have had some blood in my underpants. He told me I have a cyst on one of my ovaries and that the ovaries will have to come out and . . ." Then her voice got so quiet that he could barely understand the words, "I will not be able to have children."

Grasping the sense of her stammered words and the total grief of her tears and feelings, Don hugged her tightly. He did not fully understand what he could do or how he could help. He knew how she felt about having children, she wanted many and he accepted that need for her, asking only that they wait until they could afford them more comfortably. He had found his new job toward that purpose and was making many business connections through his busy volunteer activities in the Junior Chamber of Commerce.

"Let's sit down. Let's rest a minute here. This can't be all that bad. Maybe there is an easier answer. I will call the doctor tomorrow from the office. Let's see if there is more information then."

The next day, Don took a few minutes and called the doctor's office as soon as he could do so. The secretary said the doctor would call him back and he did so at the end of his appointments. He explained to Don the seriousness of the cyst. It was imperative that it be removed along with the ovaries because experience had proven that leaving them in could cause Dee to go insane. Don was in stunned disbelief at the idea of that happening to Dee. (Author's note: since that time, medical science has thankfully recognized that a cyst on a woman's ovaries has no influence or relation to a diagnosis of insanity.)

The doctor said he was very sorry to bear such bad news but recommended that they consider that the surgery could be done next Thursday. Don agreed, thanked the doctor, and hung up the phone. He explained to his boss that he would need to take off two days for his wife to have surgery. At his desk, he closed his eyes and dreaded the walk home to their apartment to tell her the disappointing news.

CHAPTER THIRTEEN

A few months later, it was finally a late but welcomed spring and the Romanoff's were having an outdoor gala to celebrate its arrival. Kaye had married Joe Romanoff in a monstrous snowstorm in the middle of January. Dee and Don stood up with them in the ceremony but barely made it home in a cab after the cab driver announced he could go no further. The choice was between walking two blocks or spending the night in a cigar shop, so they walked home with Don muttering all the way, thinking of Kaye and Joe on their way to Mexico for their luxurious honeymoon.

Today's springtime gala included everyone in the Romanoff's large circle of friends plus many new faces from Joe's law practice and the many organizations where he volunteered his time. Dee watched Kaye greeting guests and she was glad that Kaye seemed so happy. She wondered how long it might be before Kaye would suggest selling the modeling school. Her life with Joe was growing in many exciting directions.

Maryann Stoller joined Dee on the bench in the warm sunshine. Maryann was newly married as well. It would be two years this spring since their beautiful wedding, and she was expecting their first child. Her husband, Richard, was growing quickly in his journalism career with a nationally published magazine. It might not be too long until he became editor of one of the news divisions.

"Oh, this sunshine feels like heaven" Maryann announced, throwing her nearly bare arms upward toward her compliment. "I could just eat it up, along with all those tea sandwiches over there. I need to watch out or I'll be as big as a house in seven months!"

Dee laughed at that possibility; Maryann was the tiniest female she knew, a hair over four-foot-ten inches in Maryann's best big girl dreams.

She had sought Dee's help two years ago to find a more "grown-up " wardrobe, feeling that everything made her look like a child. They had found the perfect solutions but now, would they still fit her in a month?

"How is your sister, Mavis, lately? Is she still teaching? I haven't seen her in a good while, or Bill, come to think of it!" inquired Dee. Maryann had an older sister, much older, eight years older than Maryann and Dee. Mavis taught school and she and Bill had been married about ten years now.

"She is finishing out this year, but she has already told them she will not be coming back next fall. You know, they are still trying to have a baby, but nothing seems to be working. It breaks my heart to see her disappointment, but she has been so excited about this news," pointing to her stomach.

"She and Bill are going to try and adopt through that place in Evanston. I think it is called The Cradle. When school is out next month, she will start volunteering several days a week in the hopes that they can adopt, but . . ." and her voice dropped off, "It can take years to actually happen."

On the way home from the gala, Dee told Don about Mavis and Bill going through The Cradle to adopt a baby. He was happy for them on their plan. Don thought that was a great idea for Mavis and Bill but wondered if Dee would want to try it too. Sure enough, it was her next sentence.

"I'll call next week and look into it," he told her, but his heart was less than enthusiastic. A baby that someone else did not want was not his idea of any kind of family. It would not create a family, in his mind, just because they added someone else's child.

Years before, when Don arrived as an incoming freshman at Northwestern, he had been required to show them his birth certificate. Until that day, he had never known that his mother and father were not his real parents. No one ever told him that truth and he felt betrayed. In his eyes, it was an embarrassment to him that he would need to hide and rise above throughout his life. And when he looked back over his childhood and the distance he felt from his father now, all those feelings had a name and a reason and a coldness because he knew he was not really their son. Even if he could explain his feelings out loud, would Dee—could Dee understand them herself?

The Cradle gave them an appointment on the following Wednesday. Upon their arrival, they were escorted into Mrs. Walrath's office. She stood behind her desk but greeted them with a warm smile and shook Don's hand. She offered them comfortable chairs across from her desk. "It's a pleasure to meet you both, Mr. and Mrs. Dickinson. Please sit down and we can talk. Please tell me about what brings you to The Cradle today."

Don began his speech about being an executive at the plumbing company and how he planned to give his family a very comfortable living. Since the doctor had told them that Dee could not have children, they were looking into the possibility of adopting a baby.

Mrs. Walrath seemed delighted with that idea and explained the process of The Cradle's adoptions. There were many couples ahead of them, some of whom had already waited a few years. The Cradle, of course, had no predictions on when or how many babies might arrive in their care. They usually recommended that the prospective mother join their volunteer groups. Dee was excited about helping and said she would start as soon as she could.

Over the next several months, Dee studied through The Cradle's training course for their nursery volunteers and signed up for as many open positions available as possible, even many during the night and into the early morning hours.

She loved working with the babies and the nursing staff. Being eight years older than her next younger sister, she had grown up with plenty of hands-on experience helping her mother with baby LaVerta. Dee was well known in The Cradle for singing to the babies, especially with a fussy baby often handed to her by another volunteer.

Dee and Kaye agreed to sell their modeling business around that time. Soon after they found a buyer, they helped the new owners with many business details, ongoing project information, class schedules, and student records. She was happy to help them any way she could and hoped they would be very successful.

Almost immediately, Kaye announced that she was expecting their first child and Dee was hoping her chance to receive a baby would come at any time. She was actually delighted to sell the business as she did not want to have any other claims on her time if the opportunity arose quickly with The Cradle, and one could never tell what might happen on any day.

CHAPTER FOURTEEN

Don was at his office desk when his phone rang as he hung up the receiver from the last call. Dee was talking so fast that he could hardly make out every other word.

"Slow down! What are you saying?" he tried to get in the flow.

"Honey, The Cradle called and said they may have a baby for us! We need to be ready in six weeks, darling! Six weeks! I can't believe it. They said I do not need to volunteer after today either because they know we'll be so busy getting ready!"

"Oh, that is *wonderful* news, just wonderful. I'll try and leave the office early and we'll celebrate tonight, okay?"

"Yes, Don, that will be great. I want to call Mom first thing when you get home, too. I know it's expensive to call them long distance. I won't talk long but I just have to tell her today!"

That evening, Dee put the call through to her parents' home and her mother answered the phone. Again, Dee was talking so fast that her mother could barely make out the words but when she understood, her mother said "Praise God, Delores. Our prayers are answered, and He has saved a baby for you and Don. I will tell your Dad and your brothers and sisters. We better hang up. It will cost a lot and you have some expenses coming up! Love you, Delores."

The next few weeks were full of activity for Dee, preparing the nursery, lining up all the furniture, decorations, a highchair, a stroller, baby clothes and bottles, diapers and blankets; the list seemed endless. She would wake in the middle of the night, remembering another important item, and run to the kitchen to add it to her list.

* * *

One afternoon there was a knock at the door. Two men were holding a beautiful wooden crib as if it might be very heavy. Dee held the doors open for the men to carry in the crib and place it in the nursery—which was still in a state of chaos, stacked with supplies and boxes. The card attached to the crib exclaimed such a celebration of joy for the expectant parents and the new baby to arrive soon. Later that evening when Don arrived home from work, all he could say in his amazement was, "Golly, Mrs. Ewen."

They were told that the baby was a girl. They had to pick a name. Don considered that a girl's name was not his responsibility; whatever Dee decided would be fine as long as it was not his stepmother's first name, but Dee knew to avoid that choice.

Don's main part in the preparations was to focus on toys. Every toy he saw looked like one he simply had to have for her. He often spent his lunch hour going to the Marshall Field's department store. He knew all the latest toys and the store clerks by name. Fortunately, in their large, rented house in Evanston, the couple had plenty of space. Dee had to make an empty spare bedroom into a playroom just to hold all the toys.

The day of homecoming finally arrived, and their friend Homer drove Dee and Don to The Cradle. Homer also had another important job, running the new Bell & Howell "Two-Fifty-Two" 35mm movie camera Don bought last month. He wanted to keep the car engine running for his own sake but justified the need to have a warm car for the new baby's ride home. He was alert and watching for his cue to start the camera.

It was a crisp, chilly May afternoon but fortunately, there was very little wind as Dee and Don approached the main entrance door together and stepped inside quickly to the warm lobby area. Janet, Mrs. Walrath's secretary, was beaming in her smile when she met them and escorted them to her office. To the young couple, it felt like the whole world was smiling.

Mrs. Walrath greeted them excitedly. "Welcome again, welcome. This is always our most exciting day at The Cradle. We are so happy for all of you." Dee and Don both felt like they could not sit down for their excitement, but Mrs. Walrath said, "Please sit down and relax. It is a wonderful moment to share and enjoy." She paused and they slowly settled into the comfortable chairs "If you are ready, we will bring her in."

Dee simply nodded her head enthusiastically as she could not speak any words. Don had enough composure to say, "Certainly," but wondered how silly that probably sounded, forgetting the thought as soon as he saw the baby in Janet's arms. She paused a moment in front of them and slowly transferred the baby into Dee's arms as Dee's tears dropped silently on the blanket. There were no spoken words in the room, only indefinable words in their hearts.

Mrs. Walrath had seen this happen so many times in her years of work and never tired of its beauty. She patiently gave them time to think, feel, and speak first. Don mustered the first words, "She is beautiful," and Dee looked at him with a smiling response.

"You are now a family," Mrs. Walrath quietly reminded Dee and Don, "and she is yours."

Don looked at Mrs. Walrath as if she held the secrets of the world for the moment. "What will she be like?" he inquired.

Mrs. Walrath smiled at Don, fully understanding his wonder and curiosity. Speaking to both of them she said, "She will be what you are." Don looked back at the baby in Dee's arms, knowing all would be fine.

"Are you ready to take Susan Kaye to her new home?" inquired Mrs. Walrath, chuckling inside herself that new parents often need a comment of permission in their new roles. Don was ready, standing as if cued by the words, and Dee offered the baby in her arms to Don. He felt awkward at the moment but carefully nestled her in his left arm and talked to her with a sweet hello. Dee stood and prepared to leave for home and Don placed Susan Kaye back into Dee's arms.

"Thank you, Mrs. Walrath. Thank you." They both expressed their appreciation, and Mrs. Walrath walked with them toward the front of the building and saw them out the door, smiling. Dee and Don did not see the well of tears in the bottom of her eyes as these very special moments still never failed to tug at her heartstrings even after all the years.

Outside, Homer saw his friends come out of the building and jumped out of his driver's seat with the camera in hand. He quickly had the camera steadily rolling, capturing the happy moment. Both Dee and Don were smiling so happily, walking down the long sidewalk to the street. They were all going home.

The new nursery was decorated in a circus clown theme with all kinds of animals, a circus tent painted on the wall by Dee, and brightly colored curtains on the large sunny windows. Friends and family had helped them fill the large list of necessary supplies and Dee had sewn blankets and clothes for weeks. Mrs. Ewen had the expensive crib delivered by Marshall Fields in perfect time to begin putting it all together. Would Susan like her new bedroom?

That afternoon, they nestled Susan into her new crib with dolls and stuffed toys to keep her company. Right away, there were many phone calls and cards of congratulations, and over the next few weeks, everyone wanted to come see Susan and her new mommy and daddy.

CHAPTER FIFTEEN

Whatever doubt or fear Don had had about adopting someone else's child melted away on that first day. They settled into being a family right away. Dee became the best mother she could be and proudly walked and strolled her baby around the springtime blooming neighborhood, with Susan modeling the gorgeous outfits Dee had made.

Don learned to be a dad in his own way. He left a lot of the duties to Dee, but he took it upon himself to learn all he could. Certainly, he could handle bath time, and after a little hands-on coaching, he had accomplished his goal. It also gave Dee a chance to put her feet up after dinner. They put Susan to bed and did the dishes together. Not to be outdone by Dee's beautiful singing voice, Don spent many nights singing his favorite choice of lullaby, "Home On The Range," and it usually did the trick.

As an only child, Don had never had much contact with babies before Susan entered his world. He was amazed at all the new activities and sounds that seemed to show up overnight. Don appointed himself recorder-in-chief with his new camera and giant lighting setup, projector, and rollup screen with stand. He bought a large set of white letters to use in his work. He began a grand movie production starring his new daughter.

His first home movie opened with a big board covered in some of Dee's leftover sewing material. It copied the opening screen of any movie theatre presentation, except that Don's version featured the title of "Desuon Productions." He titled his first movie "Present - Reel One," obviously planning on multiple volumes.

In the center of the covered board, he cut out a circle, and Dee, unseen behind the board, held a stuffed lion in the background, rotating it slightly while Don ran the camera simulating the famous MGM roaring lion. Following the lion screen, he had spelled out Susan's full name using his collection of white letters against a dark background material.

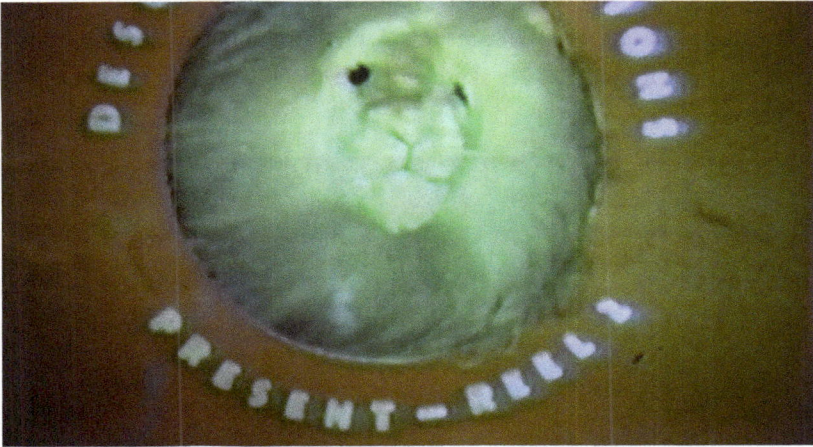

Over the years, Don filmed every possible event a child could have in her young lifetime. In the beginning, there was strolling, bottle feeding, bathing in the sink, smiling, not smiling, rolling over, standing, high-chair feeding, playpen activity, laughing, and of course, what every parent thinks is a hilarious original thought, wearing dad's hat.

To commemorate each of the moving events, he created a blank padded background with the word "CRAWLING" with his white letters, and showed a series of shots with upside-down baby shoes moving across the screen, followed by a similar version for "WALKING." He expected Hollywood to call him any day.

Reels Two and Three began with the first birthday celebration along with about a dozen kids and twice as many adults, followed by the filming of every birthday party, Easter, Christmas, visits with grandparents and cousins, dance recitals, vacations, a Halloween party, the first day of kindergarten, learning to ice skate and horseback ride, and everything in between.

CHAPTER SIXTEEN

Don had to go to a national convention in California for a week. It was located near the Disneyland Park. He wished someday they could all visit the park together but of course, for this trip, Dee had stayed home with Susan. Stopping at a souvenir shop one evening, he saw a large box of Disney pictures for sale at twenty-five cents apiece. He was unaware at the time that they were actually not just pictures, but in fact turned out to be cells used in the drawing of the Disney cartoons and movies. He could afford to buy four of them, hoping Dee would like to use them in Susan's bedroom.

They loved the "big house" that they rented in Evanston, but many families were moving to the suburbs. Like many young people, they also wanted to buy their own home. After saving enough for a nice down payment, they bought their first house in Arlington Heights, proudly adding a swing set in the backyard and a fence all the way around.

Greetings

from our house to your house

In the first spring, Don took to his gardening and landscaping responsibilities right away. Out of all the home improvements that he worked so hard to produce, he was especially proud of his rose bushes. He deemed all the impressive growth of all his plantings as a testament to his intensive study and careful research to get everything right. That pride lasted until a neighbor informed him that his house sat on what used to be a very large chicken farm and that a dead plant would grow there in the middle of winter thanks to the rich soil. Don just planted more and skipped any further research.

At an early age, Susan was bitten by a neighbor's dog. She was afraid of dogs well before the bite. Don was carrying her past the neighbor's dog because of her fear. The dog was a beautiful Dalmatian and it jumped up and bit Susan on her thigh. That made the fear even greater, that a dog could get to her anywhere, even in the safety of Dad's arms.

Rather than grow up afraid of dogs, they decided to get her a puppy. They named her Crispin's Crispian after the dog in the 1952 Little Golden Book entitled *Mister Dog*, written by Margaret Wise Brown and illustrated by Garth Williams. Interestingly, this was one of Susan's favorite books despite her fear of dogs.

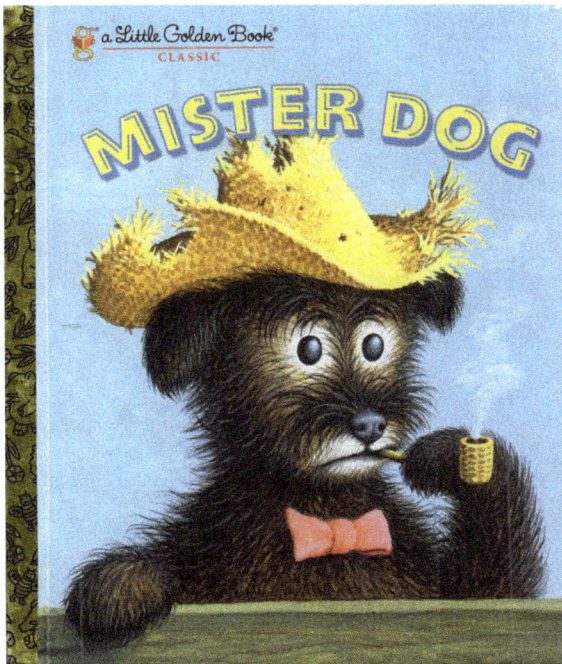

Susan and the puppy became instant pals and Susan felt no more fear toward any other dog she met—except for the neighbor's Dalmatian of course. Thereafter, Crispy showed up in every home movie and she slept on the other twin bed in Susan's bedroom. Their new friendship created love in place of fear and led to a lifetime of loving dogs rather than running from them.

Like most young couples in those days, the couple could not afford a car. Don walked two blocks to the train station to get to work at the plumbing company in Chicago. He also went to the University of Chicago at night to earn his master's degree in business. After walking home from the train station late at night in the snow, he would come into the house with icicles hanging from his brimmed dress hat and his thick eyeglasses frozen over on the lenses. Running to hug him, Susan told him, "Daddy, you smell cold." In 1956, they bought their first car, a Chevy, and it got lots of movie camera time as well.

In the late 1950s, there was an effort by the teamsters to unionize the plumbing company. It was part of Don's job to try to keep the union out of the company and present dissenting information to the employees to sway their vote against the unionization of the labor force. He was very persuasive. His background degree in psychology and his top-notch debate skills made him a formidable challenge to any forces working against his goals. He provided all the employees with honest, clear information regarding their expectations about the union. It did not look hopeful that the union would succeed.

One night, Don did not come home at the regular time and Dee did not hear from him. She was not too worried, assuming he had been delayed for work or had seen a friend on the way. Soon after, he came in the front door and she saw what had happened to cause his late arrival. His glasses were broken, and he had been hit in the jaw and beaten in his stomach and chest. In the phony setup of a proposed meeting, he had been taken to a warehouse and threatened with more if he continued to fight the union leaders. It was Chicago. All he said was "We are moving."

PART FOUR

Newport News, Virginia

CHAPTER SEVENTEEN

At this point, I think I am old enough to start telling the story by myself.

This is the first time my family has heard this story.

Like most families, they know bits and pieces and may often think that is all there is to it. Logically, we do not suspect, or we do not even guess what we do not know. We live with or around that person or persons all our lives. Don't we already know everything there is to know? What else could there be, anyway? We think we know everything.

We also assume all those answers, stories, records, memories, and the people who lived them will be here with us forever. We know in our head that all people will die someday—but we'll think about that tomorrow. Sometimes it is only after a family member is gone and we then wish we had learned so much more. What conversations should I have started in order to unlock a story? I could have asked about their pictures or the meaning of those odd treasures they kept. How many times should I have tried to pry open the window to a life?

How much do I value that laughter I felt while hearing that simple memory or story over and over? We think repetition is a guarantee that it will always be in our own memory. If we had only written it down, we might have it to enjoy today. Maybe we wish hopelessly that we could hear that one story or two just one more time and share in its laughter, or even shed some tears. Regret can be a hollow coldness to wear around our shoulders.

Dad got a job pretty quickly, working for a wholesale company that operated only in the Southern states. In fact, for some reason, he was told very explicitly that there would never be any expansion of the company above the Mason-Dixon Line. He learned all this and much more when he was brought down to Newport News, Virginia for an interview.

The company paid for the trip down and he was able to bring Mom and me along. It was a very long trip in the Chevy. We stayed in a small colonial home in Williamsburg, a short drive away from Newport News. The whole town looked like a picture book, like nothing I had seen around Chicago or even in Grandma and Grandpa's town in Michigan. There were lots of people in some kind of costumes walking all around the odd sidewalks and buildings. All the ladies had bonnets.

An interview was scheduled with the current vice president of the personnel department and the company's president. Dad went to his meeting and Mom and I walked all around the town. It was a beautiful warm day and we had lemonade for lunch. We saw horses and carriages, giant oxen hauling wagons down the street, goats and sheep eating grass on a big lawn.

The vice president came back to Williamsburg the next day and took all of us out to dinner. Mom and I returned to the colonial home early so that Dad could talk much more with the vice president. Dad was offered the position of assistant to the director of personnel. He accepted and it was agreed he would start in one month.

In his new job, Dad was charged with two duties. One was familiar to him, to keep unions from organizing in the company. The other was to develop training programs to teach people to successfully sell plumbing and electrical supplies to contractors and to the general public. It was a good match for him considering his degree in psychology and his master's degree in business. There was some possibility of advancement, maybe even to become vice president of the company someday.

After about a month, Dad drove back down to Virginia to start his new job. He lived in a hotel near the office and found a house to buy in Newport News. He sent detailed, lengthy letters to Mom over the months describing the choices of houses. Mom sold the house in Illinois, hired the movers, packed up the house, and we rode the train down to Newport News along with Crispy.

I loved the train ride. You could feel the train movement under your feet every minute, a beautiful soft rocking feeling. The musical sound of the wheels on the tracks rang in my ears all day and night. We had a tiny room with an absurdly tiny bathroom that had almost no floor in it. Everything you might need was inches away from you. In our guest room , there was a sofa and two small chairs with a table in between.

The train had a man, called a porter, who took care of us. Each night Mom and I would walk to another train car and have dinner, just like for breakfast and lunch, as well. When we were having dinner, the porter would come into our tiny room and transform the sofa into a nice bed for Mom. Above her bed appeared another bed out of the wall with a small ladder next to it. I would climb up there to sleep.

The tiny room had a gigantic window that showed us all the areas we rode through during the daytime. At first, there was a great deal of snow on the ground. It was February in Chicago when we left the train station. At the beginning of the train ride, the usual dirty black snow was piled high at every railroad crossing we passed. Soon it began to disappear, here and there. We saw the mountains and fields, thick forests, busy little towns, and the beautiful clear wintertime sunsets. At night, the window displayed a completely black screen except for the never-ending flashing city lights along the way or the stars and moonlit skies.

Every time the train stopped, the porter would tell Mom so she could walk Crispy over the two days it took to get to Newport News. Every time she walked her, the dog chain leash would tear a hole in her stocking, and she arrived in Newport News with not one wearable stocking. I was a little worried that she would miss the train and Crispy and Mom would get stuck somewhere, but the nice porter never forgot her.

The train ride was fun, but I was already missing my best friend, Katie. She had lived across the street from us in Arlington Heights and we spent many hours at each other's homes. She was an experienced horseback rider. Her bedroom wall was covered in ribbons that she had won, and I was supposed to start to learn to ride with her, maybe even with one of her two horses. Having to move away wrecked that idea but Mom promised that there would be horses in Virginia too.

CHAPTER EIGHTEEN

Moving to the South brought so many changes to all our lives in big and small ways. It was not just the oppressive heat and humidity, although their effect on us was overwhelming at times. There was no air conditioning yet. Constant perspiration was a given daily activity in the summer, limiting physical strength and energy and adding a level of drudgery to ordinary chores such as cooking, cleaning, or laundry.

Dad had a fan by his desk at work, but its meager effort could not penetrate the required suit coat, shirt, and tie. As kids, we wanted to enjoy our summer escape from school, but swimming seemed to be the only occasional refreshing playtime if we were lucky enough to go all the way to a beach. Nobody had a pool in their yard and the creek had big snakes called moccasins. Although we played by the creeks often, no one wanted to get near one of those. Often, an afternoon was only good for a nap with the quiet hum of a nearby lawnmower lulling us to dreams of cool sleep.

I was informed early on that there would be new rules of behavior which included saying "yes ma'am" and "no ma'am" and "yes sir" and "no sir." Just saying yes and no was no longer good enough. It took a while before the responses became second nature and I did not have to think about them hard to remember them. I wondered what else would change and it did not take long to see and hear about some of them, especially in my new experiences.

We rarely went out to eat in a restaurant. There just were not any restaurants around us. But when we had a special occasion, there was the Hotel Warwick downtown near Dad's office, and the Chamberlin Hotel, and we all dressed up like Sunday. Dad would not sit down until we were seated. Dad would ask Mom and me what we wanted from the menu and then he would order for us. If someone came to speak with us at our table,

Dad would stand up the whole time and introduce everyone at our table. Men never wore their hats inside and it was even frowned upon while sitting on a front porch outside, especially if a lady was present.

Mom said that a thank you note was never optional but always expected. If someone invited us to go somewhere, it was never considered an accepted invitation unless Mom approved and responded, no matter what it was. If someone stopped at our house around mealtime, it was expected that we feed the visitor as well. All of a sudden, we had an unusual plate called a relish tray because everywhere we went, there was one on that table too.

Dad had a big new change to his voice. We all noticed right away that everyone talked differently. It was almost as if they were somehow singing when they were really only talking. Mom helped Dad create his new way of talking. They called it a Southern accent. They also used another unfamiliar word all the time. Instead of "you guys" everyone said "y'all" and it seemed to cover any situation you happened to encounter.

Dad practiced with Mom until his "southern accent" sounded normal and natural. He said he could not be from the North and tell people what to do unless he sounded like them. It sounded like music to me. I soon learned that everybody talked like that, even the kids in the new neighborhood.

Dad had settled into his new office long before we arrived in town. It was already set up with a big gray metal desk and chairs and pictures on the walls. Hung on the wall behind his desk was a framed picture of the Southern states of the country, covered by a design of the Confederate flag. Next to the flag design in the picture was written "The South shall rise again!!!"

When they first showed Dad his office, he did not know what to think of that picture but was apprehensive about taking it off the wall for the time being. A coworker in the personnel department, Cliff Woods, came into his office and introduced himself warmly. After a few days, he asked Cliff about that picture.

"Cliff, are we still fighting the Civil War down here? I don't know what to think of this and I saw one of these in Larry's office too."

"Okay, Yankee" he chided him. "Sounds like you have a lot to learn about the South! Let me guess, you think it means we all want slavery to come back. Am I right?" he laughed.

"I guess I don't know what to think, yet. Tell me about it."

"First of all, nobody wants slavery to come back. Slavery was an industrial function of farming back then. It never would have lasted because of technological advancements. From the days well before the actual founding of this country, many if not most people wanted to do away with it entirely.

"You probably recall from studying history as a kid that the founders of our country debated and debated it but could not reach a majority to eliminate slavery by the delegates in the very beginning, so they put it off until they were sure they could eliminate it eventually. The sticking point was that no one knew how to run big farms and plantations without manual labor.

"Of course, we all know that Lincoln took that decision on himself by forcing the issue, and then all the agricultural states began to secede, which was their right, of course. Lincoln was afraid the country would split up completely, which in my opinion, was definitely in the process of happening. But I believe it could have and would have come back together diplomatically without a war if Lincoln had been a stronger leader—but that's just my personal thoughts.

"In the end, the South took a real beating in the Civil War. Financially, they lost everything. Most everything physical was burned to the ground or stolen. If anyone had any wealth left after the war, it was confiscated to pay exorbitant taxes or looted before any surviving soldiers could get back to their homes. General Lee negotiated strongly just to get permission for the surrendering Confederate soldiers to keep their horses to get back to their homes and keep their guns to feed themselves and their families.

"Families were ruined and broken. There were very few buildings left, industries, jobs, schools, churches, or any money to bring them back, except for rich, incoming Northerners. That picture on the wall makes a statement but it does not mean we want slavery, war, or that we have anything against Negroes. It only means that the people who loved their Southern homeland would build it back to its beauty and strength again. Can you understand their feeling?"

Don tried to understand how they may have felt after losing that long bitter war. He abhorred the concept of slavery as well, and it sickened him that some other countries in the world still practiced it legally.

"I guess so. It's not like that in the North. Other than stories and lessons in history class, I don't think anybody thought two seconds about the Civil War." Cliff could understand that but wondered if Don could truly understand the sentiment in the South, too, without misunderstanding it like so many people jumped to do.

"The North prospered greatly from the war," Cliff explained as they walked the hallway. "Their manufacturing capacity grew tremendously, and many wealthy individuals took advantage of the dire situation left in the South. That hasn't always been well received or welcomed either. Even if people lose a war, they do not necessarily lose all their pride. The South lost about a half million men. Their loved ones felt they fought with honor, despite losing in the end. Many still defend their belief today that states should make their own choices and that not everything should come from Washington, DC, as if they are some kind of monarchy."

Cliff's face had a very solemn look. "Personally, I believe that slavery itself would have been outdated in a matter of years if the politicians would have let it die of natural financial causes and technological inventions. A large part of the South had already changed their ways and there continued to be much active and ongoing debate about how to best go about eliminating slavery forever, but it never played out that way once the war started.

"That flag has nothing to do with how I feel about Black people. There will probably always be people in the world who have prejudice in their hearts. People just have to figure out a good heart for themselves. That is when good change happens. Taking a picture off a wall won't change anything at all. Remembering our history is important and we all want to make good things happen going forward." His face brightened again. "I still have faith in my fellow man. Let's get some lunch. I am starving."

As they left the office, Cliff chided Don, "You know you'll always be a damn Yankee, right?" Don looked at him hopelessly as if he might never ever win the South's acceptance, much less their affection, until Cliff finished his tease, laughing with these words: "That's a Yankee that never goes home."

CHAPTER NINETEEN

Mom had a whole new house to make into a home. It was definitely not a house she would have chosen but it did have some interesting features. She was fairly certain Don had picked it out because of the back porch. Even in the cool spring weeks, he was already enjoying sitting out there on weekends to read, one of his favorite hobbies.

The kitchen was twenty-nine feet long with all the cabinets and appliances down one wall. She thought roller skates might be handy for fixing dinner. It was in a tiny young neighborhood of two streets, located in a very rural part of town, surrounded by farms owned by Mennonites. It was several miles away from any real shopping. She quickly got to know the few neighbors and learned much more about the tiny community out in the country. It was smaller than her hometown of South Haven but a very far cry from busy Chicago and its suburbs.

The closest store was a one-room, wood-floored, two-aisle building called Briggs Grocery which was conveniently located about one mile from our house. The next closest store was about fifteen miles away, much too far away unless it was a special occasion. Mr. Briggs was the butcher and owner. Mom did all her shopping there and soon had a very high regard for Mr. Briggs' knowledge of meats and the local seafood. They would discuss the quality of cuts of meat and share cooking advice at great length.

Many of the meats and fresh vegetables that Mr. Briggs sold came from the local farmers. I loved to go to his store and wander down the very narrow aisles like a mystery maze, the high shelves stocked to the ceiling. Mr. Briggs was always in the back of the store working behind the cold meat case unless a customer needed to tally up his purchases at the small counter up front. The polished wood floors creaked with every step, and I would find the candy jar and sit outside with my treat, waiting on the front steps for Mom to finish shopping. On a very hot day, I might even get a Popsicle instead.

Artist: Jay W. Spicer

Mom loved to cook. Grits was a staple in the south and my parents caught on quickly to its rich buttery flavor. It was an absolute necessity to learn about the local seafood and one day, we went down to the local docks. Mom got out of the car and I watched her talk and laugh with the fishermen near their boats. She learned a lot from them about how to choose good fresh oysters, crabs, and clams and how to fix them. After she mastered seafood, she went on to tackle the gigantic Smithfield hams. Dad was delighted with everything she cooked, and we never had mashed potatoes once.

I missed my friend Katie but fortunately, I still had my imaginary friend Kathy. I don't really remember Kathy, but Mom and Dad laughed about her several years later, saying I would tell them she had to be dried off too after our bath, and once we even had to go back and get her at the Marshall Field's department store in Chicago.

Distance and time would diminish memories of Katie. My new friends would soon replace Kathy, too. There was Lucy who lived on the farm behind our house. Lucy was a year older, and her family was Mennonite. She was not allowed to spend the night at our house but I could stay at hers. She was not allowed to wear shorts or pants either, only dresses, and she had to wear a cap over her hair. Those differences never seemed important to us. Lucy had the best tree swing in the world, and we had hours of fun playing with our dolls.

Patty was another new friend, in fact, the only other friend. She lived across the street and she had a huge family, something very new for me to see. In her house, she had parents, a grandmother, three brothers, and a sister. It was always a busy, loud place with everyone talking at once, and it seemed like Patty's mother was always working in the house or tired. Patty spent a lot of time at my house but I loved being at hers, too.

There were more boys than girls in the small neighborhood and it was necessary to comingle if you wanted to have a decent baseball game. Patty and I drafted one of her younger brothers to make a full team of three and regularly beat all the contenders in the nearly empty yard next door.

Without a doubt, it was the very best yard on the street of houses for a baseball diamond. If truth be told, we tore it up mercilessly. Grass does not last long when you slide into bases for hours. The grownup who lived there never ever complained about the grass or clobbered, run-over bushes. That was probably our reward for not rolling our eyes when the mother would come outside and scold us for not treating their youngest boy nicely. Almost daily, he would start crying for some reason and run and tell his mother. Otherwise, we rode bikes and roller skated on driveways, played cards, jacks and board games, jumped rope, and played hopscotch.

I was sick a lot, catching measles, mumps, and everything else that went through the local school. The only doctor lived a few houses down the street and he would often stop at the house on his way home. In Chicago, I had chicken pox that turned into gangrene of the blood. Mom could not get my fever down with water or cold baths. The pediatrician was an older man of German heritage, and he told Mom over the phone, "Vutts wrong vith the beer?" And a couple of teaspoons actually worked. The neighborhood doctor would never suggest that, being Mennonite, but he laughed at Mom's story.

I did not know anyone else who got sick all the time, only me. I missed a lot of school because it was important to not spread the germs to other kids. If it was a pretty day and I was not too sick, Mom and I would go fishing down at the lake. Grandpa made us some bamboo poles when he and Grandma came for a visit.

Mom would pack us a little picnic lunch and we would fish all day. Mom did not like to clean the fish, but Patty's grandmother did a fine job and Mom would cook them for dinner. One time she was baiting her hook and it went into her thumb. We had to leave all our fishing gear and go to the local doctor's office. He fixed it up and gave her a tetanus shot. Unfortunately, she had a reaction to that right away. We got home at the same time Dad got home from work and had big stories to tell about our day.

Growing up, I always knew I was adopted, as far back as I can remember. It was just a word and I never really thought of it as different in any way. Being around Patty's and Lucy's families seemed somehow different though in a way I had not felt around Katie and her parents in Illinois, but then Katie was also an only child. I could not define the different feeling; I could only sense that something was different, not wrong, just different.

CHAPTER TWENTY

Although based on looks I could have been a fill-in for Shirley Temple, to my mother's disappointment, I had no singing voice, and the dance recitals were documented proof that I had no gift for dance. I was also as introverted and shy as a turtle, never a leader but a staunch second fiddle if you needed a pal.

I wasn't a total tomboy, but I hated the frilly itchy dresses that she loved to make or buy. I had pairs of fancy ruffled pants and insisted on wearing them backward so I could see the pretty lace ruffles and they also did not seem to itch much that way. I had several petticoats. One solid consolation prize was that Mom would use leftover material and always make matching outfits for my Betsy McCall doll.

As the neighborhood grew with many new houses being built, it also grew in friends. Mom's friend from college moved in down the street. She was from New York City and had a new husband, Howard, with her as well as three children. Her oldest child was a girl named Jacky, then the oldest girl in the neighborhood. Her stepfather, Howard, was a nice man but he and Jacky butted heads on nearly every subject. In fact, Jacky could butt heads with almost anyone. Fortunately, she had other glowing attributes for all of us around our neighborhood. She always had ideas. She always knew what we could do for fun—and we followed her ideas everywhere.

By this time, there were plenty more girls added to our group: Missy, Marny, and Lisa. We created sizable dirt forts on the vacant house lots to fight off the boys just in case they invaded. We climbed trees and built tree houses, ran all through the woods nearby, and watched out for snakes. While we were out and about the neighborhood, we would eat lunch at one of our homes, whichever one was closest when the hunger pains hit, and empty out a loaf of bread and a jar of peanut butter.

Jacky always had a story to add purpose to our daily roaming. She had tales of life in New York City and life with a father who had been mean and cruel. She gave her stepfather, Howard, credit for not being like her real father had been. She had stories of blizzards and big cities and lots of strange people, all of which were completely foreign to our limited world experiences. We were in awe.

One day, Jacky's mother called my mother and asked if I would come down to visit her. When I got to her house, her mother answered the door and led me to the hallway bathroom. Jacky was naked in a full bathtub, covered in red blotches and her eyes were shut. She had gotten into some poison ivy. For the first time, I had to entertain *her*, and it was a daunting task. I went to her room and got books and I read to her the rest of the day. We sang songs and told funny stories. The cool bath water alleviated some of the itching and I alleviated some of her boredom.

Howard's mother, Gram, lived nearby on a large "farm." They called it a farm but I never saw what they grew. Gram lived alone in a huge, very old house and we loved to go visit her every chance we could. We never went upstairs but the first floor held so many mysteries that we really did not need any more intrigue.

There was a large white barn that was filled with every conceivable thing that a farm might have. It also held items that seemed like they should be in the house instead of the barn, like lampshades and a few big chairs. It prompted hours of exploring for us and we would beg Gram to tell us why it was there, what was it for, and if we could use it for something else like our latest magnolia tree house.

Inside the house, there were just as many curiosities. The living room was filled with piles of old books and statues, and it always looked to me like they might be moving. Several boxes were always half open or stacked on furniture. There were pictures of people we never saw around the house—except for the big one over the fireplace. You could tell it was Howard as a young kid but it was impossible to really picture him being that little. Gram had a bedroom behind the living room but we thought she never slept. She was always in her kitchen or reading a book all night.

The only living thing in the big white barn was a horse. She was a beautiful, tall chestnut retired cavalry horse incompatibly named Lady. It was hard to picture "Lady" going into fierce battles in a cavalry. Although Lady was supposed to be retired, we were thrilled to ride her all over the farm together.

Lady was so big that we had to stand on a block to get on or even to put her bridle on. Fortunately, she was so patient with our slow efforts to get her bridled and saddled and she never moved an inch until we said go. The saddle had a hole in the seat for something and many days we just skipped it and rode bareback together.

A large, completely window-covered porch surrounded the entire house and was also filled with mysteries. The porch had two beds that Gram mysteriously called daybeds even though we never slept in them in the daytime. That is where we always slept when Jacky and I visited the farm. Gram called it the sleeping porch.

The house had no air-conditioning, and the summers were very hot. The sleeping porch was on the shady side of the house, flanked by giant magnolia trees. Gram would lower the porch windows from the top and the black ceiling fans ran all the time. In our hours of whispering late into the night before falling asleep, we were oblivious to the heavy sweet smells of the summer gardenias and lilacs next to the porch. We slept like babies, listening to the frogs and night creatures as long as we could.

I think Jacky loved Gram more than anyone in her life. I'm not sure why. They just clicked. Jacky seemed to be happier at the farm than anywhere else. We had many days of talking to Gram while she worked in her small kitchen, watching her trim some fresh vegetables or bake cookies. She never let us help her, but she seemed to like our company.

Like everything else about Jacky, no subjects were untouchable. If she had any kind of question, and she always had a question, it seemed to pop right out of her mouth. We talked about everything in the world, in our world anyway, even about me being adopted. In fact, it fascinated Jacky much more than it did me. She could take any information and make it into a great mystery.

"What if your real mother is a great queen somewhere? Maybe she is a movie star!" she would insist. Gram just chuckled. "You really need to find out who it is. How can we do that Gram?"

"Jacky, that is up to her parents, not us. Besides, she does have a Mom and Dad, you know."

Jacky, undaunted by that fact, said to me, "Tell Gram what you know already. Listen Gram . . ."

"I was born in Chicago, and they got me through an adoption place called The Cradle. I guess I was a baby. That's all. One day I asked Mom for a brother or a sister, but The Cradle told Mom and Dad that I would be enough for them." Gram chuckled again, never stopping her work on the table.

"I think you should write to that place and see if they will tell you anything else." Jacky always had the ideas and the plans.

CHAPTER TWENTY-ONE

Everything outside our world was a long way away, literally. It took about an hour for Dad to get to his office and he refused to drive fast. Sometimes I wondered if we were even moving. He had a company car now and he could not bear the idea of having a ticket or an accident.

Several of the other men at his office would kid him because they said they could stop at the gas station, the liquor store, and the cleaners and still beat him home. Dad just smiled and laughed with them, but he knew he would have to reprimand another coworker if that employee was caught speeding or had an accident with a company car. In his eyes, that would be impossible for him to do if he acted the same way or drove carelessly.

I had a new school that was also far away, so I rode with Dad in the early mornings and he dropped me off on his way to work. The new school did not have a school bus. In the afternoon, I rode home on the city bus which dropped me off at Briggs Grocery. I said hi to Mr. Briggs and then sat on the steps until Mom came to pick me up. We still had one car, the Chevy, until they decided Mom needed a station wagon, a very cool car that had lots of room. Mom was never allowed to drive the company car.

That company car came with many more responsibilities for Dad. The company was expanding into several parts of the South, opening branches in many small towns, and it was Dad's job to set up the managers and new employees. He was gone from home a lot of the time. During the summer months, Mom and I could go with him, so we got to see a lot of small towns and highways.

Being from up North, we all began a love affair with the South in general and never looked back, relishing in the beauty, the casual, slow simplicity and gentleness we saw all around us, most often represented in the sweet-sounding slow dialects of many different regions. Someone from fifty miles away could have a completely different accent and it was just as beautiful. However, sometimes it was much harder to understand what they were saying.

We celebrated the South's rich history, the foods, and the generations of people, all of whom claimed to be distantly, rather miraculously, somehow related to General Robert E. Lee. The South surrounded us with its love and we loved it back. On our summertime journeys, Mom would pack us picnic lunches to get us to our destinations. Everything that came out of that wicker basket was a surprise. Even the thermos bottles had hot coffee for Dad and ice-cold lemonade for me. She and I would see the towns as Dad worked all day.

Dad also had to do a lot of hiring at the home office. If it was a manager position, he had to take the prospective employee out to lunch. For that occasion, he was given a membership in the local country club and he charged the meals to the company. Like everything else, it was so far away that we rarely went there for fun, but Mom wanted me to take swimming and tennis lessons. Having been a lifeguard, she would never let me grow up without being able to swim, at least enough to keep myself from drowning.

I learned more about tennis from Dad. He had taught himself in college by watching other players and he was so good that he earned extra money by hustling tennis with his fellow college boys. He had notches all over his racket press indicating all his big wins. Of course, he didn't hustle players at the country club, but I bet he could have.

With me being in school most of the day, Mom had a new freedom of time. She had her friend from college, Jacky's mom, and they knew other ladies in the neighborhood. One day they all piled in a car and drove to the nearby town of Williamsburg. It had been the first capital of our country, and a very wealthy man began an organization to save and restore its historical buildings. He knew that the history of the founding of our country was worth preserving.

The ladies had heard all about the town, Colonial Williamsburg, and knew that the organization he had started was hiring so they all applied for the job of escort. To their delight and surprise, they were all hired on the spot.

* * *

At home, we had a third bedroom which we called the den. It had a sofa, chairs, and our black and white television. Mom took everything out of the large den closet and filled it with about one hundred thick spiral notebooks. Their first job as escorts was to read, study, and memorize and they were paid to do so at home, intensely going through hours of reading all those notebooks. They would all be tested.

As escorts, the ladies were required to know every fact about the founding of the country, the complete lineage of Great Britain's royal family, every fact of the biographies of the founding fathers, every plant that existed back then, and their Latin names, every aspect of colonial life such as businesses and trades, education, laws, and churches. Mom had to know everything there was to know just in case any visitor asked any question at all.

Needless to say, the husbands were not exactly thrilled with this idea of working. During that time, most wives did not work outside the home and stayed busy with raising children and taking care of home duties. Children came home after school or stayed home if they were sick. As Mom used to say, if you want to have children, why would you have other people raise them?

If a wife worked outside the home, many men felt that it would reflect poorly on them, implying that they were unable to support their family alone. There were many career women already in the general workplace, but it was a gradual development and still a matter of elective choice in many cases.

But the ladies had a plan, hoping that all the husbands would give it a try. Dad agreed to try it when he heard that they could use the extra money for some new golf clubs. Howard would get that new paint job for his old Chrysler. Another husband, Jim, was hoping for a short vacation, any vacation at all. As long as nothing changed otherwise in their world—this was the condition they all required. (Of course, darling!) The plan just might work.

CHAPTER TWENTY-TWO

After several weeks of reading and studying, the ladies passed their testing and became escorts. Under agreement with most school boards in Virginia and some in North Carolina, buses of fourth-grade school children came to Colonial Williamsburg on day-long field trips. An escort would spend the day with each busload of children, teaching them about the foundation of their country, its Revolutionary War, and the separation from England's rule.

The young children learned all about how much work, debate, and thought went into creating a whole new country based on a brand-new concept, individual freedoms that come from God, not simply handed down by a king. They realized quickly how hard it was for all thirteen different colonies to agree on even the simplest topics, how hard it was for many of them to keep everyone together long enough to iron out their arguments and keep listening to each other. It would not be a perfect beginning, but the people, the citizens, would have the power to improve it as they went along. That was something no other country had ever had.

The escorts would ride on the buses and guide the school groups through the colonial town, always beginning with the Capitol building and then visiting various other places, constantly talking with the children and walking all day. The children often asked questions as they heard the stories of their country's history. The escorts walked so much that Colonial Williamsburg gave them a shoe allowance.

The children's tours always ended in time for the ladies to be home and meet their own children after school. The visiting groups often still had hours of travel time to return to their hometowns. No doubt many of the visiting school children slept on their school bus rides home after a very long day.

That schedule worked out fine for my family during the school year while I was in school most of the day. In the summer months, I was still too young to stay home by myself all day, so I went to work with Mom.

On some workdays, I could ride on the touring school buses with her and listen to her stories over and over. On other days, I could ride the free Colonial Williamsburg buses around the town by myself with two dollars in my pocket for lunch at the drugstore counter downtown. I had open access to any of the buildings in the colonial capital because of Mom's job.

On beautiful summer days, I would often sit in the colonial gardens behind the buildings and read or draw pictures or walk over and watch the blacksmith in his shop or the wigmaker making a wig. On a rainy day, I would watch the free movie "The Story of a Patriot" ten times in the Information Center. It was a fictional tale of a man who had to choose between continuing to live in the American colonies under the tyranny of the British king or supporting the revolutionary efforts to create a new country based on individual rights and freedoms.

As long as I stayed on the Colonial Williamsburg buses and in the colonial town itself, of basically one long street, it was like a giant fairy tale with costumed players and stories galore. Sometimes, toward the end of a day, I would sit in the Raleigh Tavern bakery just for the wonderful intoxicating smells while watching the men make bread and gingerbread cookies. If I had enough money left over, I would buy us two cookies, and Mom and I would eat them on the way home.

Mom and her friends continued to be escorts for many years. When an escort excelled at her tours over time, she was promoted to escort other types of tour groups such as high school or college students, teachers, or special groups who requested specific topics of discussion such as architecture or fabrics, for example. The highest advancement was to escort visiting dignitaries or elected politicians from our country or foreign countries.

After several years, Mom graduated to the highest level of visitors and met many famous people, but she always spoke fondly of her tours of fourth graders. She said the children still had open minds and were eager to learn about the birth of their freedoms and individual rights. Unfortunately, she said, the dignitaries often had already made up their minds about their world and they had no interest in learning about the past.

After about ten years of working in Colonial Williamsburg, Mom began to lose her voice a lot. She guessed it was from all that talking and teaching. She sounded fine to me but she even said she'd lost her singing voice. I was busier than ever with school projects and needed more of her time. She left her world of work behind her and focused more on her home. She became active in the local garden club, helped with volunteering in her community, played golf with her friends, and took it upon herself to paint and redecorate the house . . . again.

Dad's job was very demanding of his time and even when at home, he worked on training programs, writing meeting formats, or endlessly analyzing benefits packages for employees. He traveled almost constantly as the company grew from fifteen branches to over eighty throughout the South. Many times he would come home to a newly painted or wallpapered room but was too tired to even notice a change.

The 60s and early 70s were a historic time for growth in the South. With many companies being forced to meet government-ordered racial quotas, Dad was immersed in the ever-evolving employment laws. He agonized over having to hire and fire people simply because of their skin color. He was forced to constantly explain a system he did not design or believe in which promoted or passed up people for indefensible reasons.

One of the very best parts of his job was hiring new employees and he was very happy to hire anyone qualified for any position, but he vehemently resented the government and certain political celebrities ordering and threatening many employers. His instincts told him that their ideas were never about fairness. Their goal was all about power, power over people they were convinced were helpless to succeed if relying on their own merit. When he hired a black person for any position, Dad chose the person based solely upon their credentials and made a point of complimenting them.

In spite of his dedication to complying with the governmental commands, and although he always supported integration, he confided to Mom his frustration of being forced to steamroll a change over other people's lives.

"It makes everything worse and then nobody is happy, even the man I hired yesterday!" he told Mom. "The only result of all this seems to be that everybody now resents everybody else. I would say Washington, DC treats us like children but it's worse than that. People are not cattle to be herded around through their lives and communities for the sake of a national headline or political votes. Real life and human beings are not a textbook paragraph."

Everyday human life is all about choices and consequences. In most cases, there are no winners when you take away someone's freedom of choice. You also take away the consequences and the learning that comes from both. Most people dislike the feeling of being manipulated or played. When people resent being ordered to do things, they resist much more than they ever would have had they been left to decide on their own terms and in their own time. "Love can't run through a heart of resentment" was Mom's response.

The very real and cruel practice of segregation was a quiet rule in the South and even more quietly existing in the North. Like many quiet rules, it wasn't mentioned and rarely questioned, just obeyed. My parents never thought about Black people being lesser than them. It was just not the way they were raised to think.

In the Tidewater area at that time, many of the Blacks lived in different locations than Whites. The same design existed in the North, though the North wanted to say it was different. The Blacks were all still in the community, just nearby, shopping at the same stores but not going to school together until that was forced by governments as well. Our city's school district was a long narrow peninsula of land. The children from one end of the city had to ride to school for an hour to get to the opposite end and no one was happy about that "solution" either.

America will never know if the South would have changed its quiet rules on its own without being forced and threatened. Throughout the South's history, the government repeatedly decided that they were not doing everything fast enough and took that choice away from them. There were already many people, employers, churches, schools, and organizations that were creating small changes and improvements on their own for all the right reasons, through love, understanding, and growth.

There is another advantage to small changes. With small changes, big change can be seen as possible and thereby be successful. But a person can't just see something with their eyes and call that changed; they must be able to see it with their heart and only when their heart is ready. The South will never be credited with the changes it made by itself. Forever after the Civil War, the South would be charged and convicted of the guilt of never doing the right thing about racism fast enough for the rest of the country's opinion. In many people's eyes, the South would never ever be good enough. I believe you needed to have lived in the South at that time to understand all the factors.

* * *

Dad was told by one of his coworkers that Mom should have a maid to help her with the house. Mom said she did not need a maid. In compliance with some other quiet rule, she got one anyway so that Dad could say yes to his boss. He walked a fine line being from the north and he would pick and choose what he could resist and what he would coalesce.

In truth, Mom was never the best housekeeper. A beautiful day was for dusting off the fishing poles, or we might take off for a ride in the countryside. Bernice came to "help us" one day a week and she did help out a lot. She was great fun, too, with lots of stories. She had lunch with us when she came to work at our house, probably against some other quiet rule. It was referred to as "quiet" only because social rules were often simply accepted without question. As children, we do not always get a clear understanding of our world until we are older. To me, Bernice was just a guest in our house. Quiet rules can also quietly disappear without anyone seeing them go. Many people in the South made change happen, quietly.

I was really hoping that I might get out of doing the ironing and my other chores but that was only wishful thinking. In fact, besides Mom's list of chores, Bernice gave me some more. A neighbor told Mom that I was spoiled. I sure wanted to show the lady my list of chores and compare it to her kid's list.

Not long after Bernice's first grandbaby was born, we drove her home after work and went inside to see the new baby and bring her a gift. Mom was permitted to hold the baby and exclaimed at how beautiful she was. When it was time for us to leave, she thanked them for having us visit. On the way home, Mom said again how beautiful she was.

CHAPTER TWENTY-THREE

When it came time for me to go to college, of course, Mom and Dad wanted me to go to Northwestern. There was a lot of unrest on college campuses all over the country. They took me to visit Northwestern, hoping I would fall in love with the idea. What stood out to me were all the graffiti-covered walls and the grungy-looking people sitting and lying around the school buildings. Windows had been broken and were boarded up in a halfhearted repair.

Mom and Dad were horrified. An editorial in the school newspaper decried the efforts of the school administration to punish the vandalizing students. Mom quoted her days from Colonial Williamsburg, saying one person's rights leave off when they infringe on another person's rights. No one had the right to damage school property, no matter what they thought. I did not have to tell my parents I did not want to go there to school, but I applied anyway.

Although I spent many curious hours wondering who my natural parents were, I never really pursued their identities. My parents were always open about the only information they had received at the time. Their documents included a copy of the court's adoption decree and my birth certificate, which only showed Mom and Dad's names as my parents. The court's adoption decree showed a woman's name of Elizabeth Cobb, as my natural mother.

Mom told me that a fraternity brother of Dad's had handled the adoption legalities for them. She doubted if the name was supposed to be on their copy of the decree and that it was probably an error. All adoption records in the state of Illinois were "sealed" by the court with the intention that no one would ever see the real parties involved.

With that limited knowledge, I simply went about my life of colleges, marriages, jobs, and the birth of one child. It was then, after my daughter's birth, that I began to think more seriously about my ancestry. I began to search for an Elizabeth Cobb all over the country, starting around the Chicago area and moving outwards to all points north, south, east, and west. I wrote letters and made phone calls based on city phone books.

The "Elizabeth Cobb" receivers of my phone calls were certainly shocked to have a question like mine out of the blue. There was no easy way to say it other than "Hi, did you happen to give up a baby for adoption?" Most of them took the shock pretty well but they could not help me with any answers. One lady said, "Sorry kid. It ain't me."

Many people responded generously with letters or notes of sympathy and encouragement, but no answers were included. I was beginning to wish Elizabeth could have had a crazy spelling for a last name. Although I did not know a single one personally, there seemed to be millions of Cobbs.

National organizations in support of more open adoption information began to form. Adoptees could register with them in case one of their biological family members might be searching for them. A few of the organizations would compare pieces of similar information in an effort to recognize a possible match. Although their newsletters showed many success stories with pictures of people who looked very much alike, they never contacted me with any match.

There were several books on how you could locate people, mostly through DMV records or state birth or marriage records. I contacted all fifty states because I did not know where she lived. Unfortunately, since I only had a woman's name, I was limited to not knowing where or when she was born, or if Cobb was a married or maiden name. Nothing came out of the fifty states.

Over the years, I would get excited about searching, follow up on a new idea, hear of a new organization, or talk to others about the search in general. In many ways, any searching was very time-consuming and often expensive for postage, phone calls, and stationery.

When you are young and busy with life in general, jobs, and family, there isn't a lot of thinking or working time for hobbies—and that is how I treated my search, like a hobby. I had boxes of copies of correspondence and information and it stayed at the bottom of my closet for many years, reappearing if a new idea arose literally out of nowhere.

At some point, I began to think about all the people who actually knew the answers I was seeking. Real people did know all the facts and names and information that I was floundering around in the dark to find. Real people did know the truth. Maybe it couldn't hurt to ask after all. What would I have to lose?

The legal proceedings had been handled by Dad's old fraternity brother, Max, from college. I started with him and wrote a letter asking if he could remember anything about my natural parents. He was kind enough to call me. He was actually a patent attorney, but he handled the adoption as a favor to my parents. He could not remember any details, never met the other parents, and said that digging up any old paperwork would not tell me any more than what I already knew.

Then I decided to track down the doctor who delivered me. His name was on my birth certificate. Through the American Medical Association, I was able to find where he was still practicing medicine and I wrote to him. He was generous enough to send me a very nice note saying he had delivered hundreds of babies and could not recall any details about my own. It was certainly a reasonable response, and my obviously non-stellar entry into the world could not compete in the memory books with hundreds of babies. He said the Cook County Hospital would have all the old records as he had been employed by them at that time.

Cook County Hospital was looking like a sure bet for a wealth of information just ready for the taking. Surely, they would release my own records. I called to find out what was necessary and where to mail my request. The woman told me they would not release birth information to a child, only to the birth mother herself and I should ask my mother to make the request. I avoided telling the woman that I had been given up for adoption, making that plan impossible and I hung up the phone with dismay.

I told Mom about all my efforts. She said that they always guessed Elizabeth Cobb may have been a student at Northwestern or the University of Chicago who just had an unplanned pregnancy. It seemed like a good possibility so I contacted those schools, but there was no student listed under that name for that time period or anywhere close to it.

It seemed that all roads were dead ends and invisible barriers were everywhere, almost as if invisible people were waiting for me to try different areas while laughing at my futile efforts. I wrote a letter to the hospital and forged the name of Elizabeth Cobb requesting a copy of her own medical records. A few weeks later, I received a response, saying they were sorry but the records had been lost in a large flood several years before and could not be retrieved. I also took it as a sign that I should avoid forgery in the future.

I was angry at the circumstances, angry at the state of Illinois which made decisions and, in my opinion, callous laws resulting in no recourse for the human beings subjected to them. I felt as if I was less than a helpless stray dog at the dog pound and I was very resentful of that nameless, faceless system that made all these decisions without my consent.

It felt as if everyone involved had legal rights, protections, and choices except for me and I was the pawn in their giant chess game. There was no one to even complain to and even if I did, I felt completely powerless to have them listen or ever understand. I wrote a blistering letter and sent it to the editor of the Chicago Tribune. I never heard a response and doubt very seriously if they ever printed it.

CHAPTER TWENTY-FOUR

I needed to calm down and step away from the "hobby" of discovering my biological family. I concentrated on my own family and the busy life we were all living. I was extremely blessed and needed to remember all the blessings around me. I had a wonderful husband, a beautiful daughter, loving and devoted parents, a good job, good health, and good friends. I was nearly thirty years old.

Some friends and family members questioned my interest in researching my past, cautioning me that there was a possibility that the answers could be very unhappy discoveries. Some of them indeed had family histories that concerned them personally, such as mental illness, criminal behavior, or disturbing lines of their medical history. Perhaps I was better off not knowing rather than living with the fear that those kinds of negative influences might affect me as well—or my daughter, in particular.

As a result of my searching, would I be passing along only negative, damaging information to my daughter or future generations? What if any newly found family members needed money? Would I be able to deny helping them? We were not wealthy, comfortably meeting our needs, but we did lead a fairly conservative financial lifestyle compared to many of our friends.

They all had valid points that were worth considering, but they also knew without any doubt who their biological families were. It was a given fact, something they never needed to wonder about or question. It was all there for them to see and hear about from day one. They looked like Grandma or Uncle Jimmy, laughed just like Jennifer, and were smart like Jack.

In my adopted life, I was never ever treated as though I were different, unloved, or not part of my extended adoptive family. They were my family and always would be, no matter what. But the reality was that I did not look like anyone in my family.

Listening to their concerns about the hazards of digging up my past, I completely understood their points and I truly was most grateful that they cared enough about me to help me weigh all sides, but the tug of curiosity on my heart was stronger than their arguments for caution.

They were quick to quote that popular expression of "having 20-20 hindsight." Unfortunately, it is only after a person finds the answers that they know right then that they should have stopped the searching and left well enough alone. Then it is too late, the horse is out of the barn, and the genie is out of the bottle.

Of course, then again, the thought always came back to the fact that just maybe a person could find out nothing but good news, and so they keep trying, eternally optimistic. I consoled myself and dismissed any real fear. After all, there were many celebrities who had adopted children from The Cradle, such as Bob Hope and Roy Rogers. Maybe other celebrities had also given up children through The Cradle and maybe I really was related to someone famous. The elusive, undefined image and the mystery held much more romance for me than apprehension.

I knew The Cradle could not release any names to me but at this point, I had to try to contact them in some way. All the information seemed locked in their domain. Perhaps there would be some clues in whatever they said. They did not know that I knew the name of Elizabeth Cobb and I would not tell them.

I sent a nice letter of curiosity asking for anything they could share. I was utterly amazed at their extremely patient and warm response. Their letter read:

My dear,

It is always a treat to hear from our Cradle children. It is especially gratifying when a letter reads as yours, that you have had a good life. That is what your birth mother wanted for you because she was not in a position to keep you. Adoption had to be her plan.

We will certainly share your natural background with you except for names and locations. Adoption decrees in Illinois continue to be impounded, so identifying information is confidential and given only by court order.

But let me satisfy some of the curiosities you have. Your birth mother was 29, and had completed high school when just 17. When employed she was a teletype operator. She was an only child and her father, your natural maternal grandfather died when your birth mother was young. His death was the result of a car accident. Your grandmother went into a Real Estate job and successfully gave good average advantages to your birth mother. There was good health history and we have no record of hereditary illness.

Physically, your mother stood 5 feet, 5 ½ inches and was slight in build. She had medium brown hair, brown eyes and fair skin. She was American born as were her parents and their origin was of mixed English strains.

Your natural father was 36, American born and he too was from English origin. He had good health and had been in the 2nd World War for 5 years. When honorably discharged, he was a supervisor in a post office. His parents were deceased, but we have no record of the causes of their deaths.

Physically, your natural father was slender and stood 6 feet, 1 inch. He had brown hair, light blue eyes and fair skin. He had had a high school education. Both your natural parents were Protestant.

As for your health, you were well from birth. You were full term and your birth mother had no infections during her pregnancy.

You were delivered spontaneously after an easy 12 hours, 50 minutes. You weighed at birth 5 pounds, 12 ounces. In length, you were 47 centimeters. All tests were negative.

In The Cradle nursery, where you stayed 50 days, you were an alert infant, always hungry, doing well, and you left in good condition.

Maybe you will feel better satisfied about yourself after this letter. We hope so. Should you have further questions, feel free to write again.

Please greet your parents for us and to all three of you, our warm wishes.

Sincerely,
MK

Suddenly, the people who conceived me and walked away were now real people, with brown hair like mine, with parents of their own, and jobs and everything. They went to high school. They had lives. I could almost picture them. My mind willingly filled in any missing pieces on their smiling faces.

But why were they so old? Why had I always pictured them as young and careless? Every piece of information would contribute to building real people and open up more and more questions. I was a long way from being satisfied. It was more like holding a bone in front of a hungry dog.

CHAPTER TWENTY-FIVE

Over the next few years, there were occasional rumblings of big potential legal changes as a few states began to loosen their tight grip on court-held adoption records. New adoptions became more open in general between all parties, welcoming an understanding that shared knowledge can promote a healthy starting point.

Opening-up information for new adoptions was simple enough to do, but the question left standing was how to open very personal and emotional pasts that involved legal contracts of privacy that were not easily broken once those promises were made.

Several newspaper and television stories showed the dangers of haphazardly and carelessly releasing private information such as grown children showing up on a birth parent's doorsteps out of nowhere and possibly forcing an entire family into chaos. The reverse event occurred in Ohio where a birth parent stalked an adoptee and asked for money from the family.

Another issue in the mix was when the birth parent was already deceased and therefore could not change their mind or speak up to hold fast to their original choice of complete privacy. Legitimate concerns and fear of the worst possible outcomes stalled changes in many states' laws.

To its credit, The Cradle held fast to its fiduciary duty to privacy and indeed Illinois itself would become one of the last states to open any records at all. Mindful of the onslaught of correspondence from all parties, The Cradle did begin a creative new option for their adoptees and birth parents. They began a registry in-house.

Any adoptee or biological parent could register with The Cradle's registry if they desired to participate in communication with the other party. When there was a match between parties, they were required to participate in individual, separate counseling through The Cradle. After completion of the counseling, they could meet or communicate only in the company of The Cradle counselors. It was a start and a very smart start.

In response to one of my letters of questions to The Cradle, they kindly refused to provide the "identifying information viewed by Illinois law" and offered forms for the new Cradle Adoption Registry. This was in 1987.

I sent the completed forms off right away but over the following years, there was never an inquiry from either of my birth parents to complete the plan of communication. Of course, the questions in my mind were, what if they did not know about the registry opportunity? How could they register to meet me if they don't know about it? Or did they just not care?

While still somewhat hopeful that their registry might work out well for me, I continued to ask questions of The Cradle and their patience was exemplary. There was never a form letter from them with a box checked or a scribbled note allowed on an optional blank line. A response might take several days or more, but it was always a personal typed letter that addressed every question I had asked.

My inquiry in 1993 was about my copy of the adoption decree itself. I still did not admit that I had her name on my copy. It felt like the only high card in my poker hand. In the decree, the birth mother was called the "sole surviving parent." Did that mean the birth father was dead? The response in their return letter read:

"The wording on your adoption decree "sole surviving parent" does not mean your birth father was dead. He was alive at the time of your birth and adoption, but he was not considered your legal father because your birth parents were not married to each other. In the eyes of the law in 1953, any child who was born outside of marriage was considered to have only one legal parent, that is the child's mother."

So, it was an affair. I was the result of an affair. The wording in the letter from The Cradle—*were not married to each other*—said it all. It did not say "they were unmarried" or "they were not married." He must have been married and she was not. She couldn't possibly be married at that time. How could she be married, have an affair, and hide nine months of pregnancy from any husband?

My mind was trying to second-guess roads into uncharted territory, pondering a large variety of possible combinations based on only my now super-hyped imagination. And if he was married, did he even know about me? Did he have other children? It was a bit exhausting to think about, contemplating how or when or why it all happened. At some point, it all went back into the bottom of the closet, simmering silently.

CHAPTER TWENTY-SIX

A couple of years later, I wrote another letter to The Cradle requesting "medical and social information." Essentially, I was asking them to open up the same file of information on me but each time I asked a new type of question. Unless I asked the right question, I would not get any more information out of that small file. But this time, they sent a boat-load.

With their response, they attached several photocopies of the medical records covering the activities in the hospital, followed by the notes from The Cradle Nursery where I lived for several weeks after birth. The copies contained lists of medical details that appeared fairly routine and normal, such as the character of the birth mother's delivery, descriptions of feeding schedules, blood tests, and laboratory results documentation.

Reading further down the page, the typed form from Cook County Hospital showed a section entitled "Family History" about the birth mother which read:

Infections during pregnancy? *None* was written in the blank.

Is this mother's first pregnancy? *No*

If not give number of children living: "3" was written originally in the blank and someone then changed it to a "2."

Whoa! There was another pregnancy before me? Could that mean that I would have a sibling? My mind was jump-started in the next second, like a cable going from one battery to another. Did that mean I could actually have a sister or a brother?

I wrote back to The Cradle that day. If I had not lived four states away, I would have driven over and knocked on the door. Did my birth mother keep the other one or two children before I was born? Was it the same birth father? It only took a few weeks to receive more answers which as always, created new questions. The Cradle wrote back:

"In regard to the records, we cannot say if there were actually two pregnancies before your birth pregnancy, only that it does appear that someone at the hospital did change the response from a "3" to a "2," and the letter continued:

"In regard to the daughter that was born to your birth mother from a marriage that ended in 1943: Your birth mother was raising her first born child at the time of your placement. This first child is your half sibling. Her father was your mother's first husband. Your birth father was a different man. Your birth mother and half-sister shared the same last name at the time of your placement."

I was dumbfounded. I had never seriously wished for a sister or brother. Being an only child did have some great advantages. Having a fairly independent nature, I never felt lonely or bored without a sibling. The fights I witnessed between my friends' siblings did not look like fun to me. Often, they were very jealous of each other. Reading those few lines in this letter from The Cradle changed all that. It would no longer be a hypothetical thought. I instantly had a sister, a real one, some-where.

The image of an older sister started to form in my mind. She was a much older sister already, at least ten years older, maybe even more. So apparently, Elizabeth was unmarried at the time and already had a half-grown child and had to give me up because it would be too expensive to raise another child. I told myself that anyway. It did make sense unless she was somewhat wealthy.

Leaping forward from here, how would I now find this new person, my new sister, with a last name of Cobb, no first or middle name, an unknown birth date, and an unknown birthplace? That seemed even more daunting than finding an Elizabeth Cobb somewhere in the Unit-ed States.

Then The Cradle made me an offer.

CHAPTER TWENTY-SEVEN

Public sentiment for adoption cases, particularly for the adoptee children, was now evolving fairly rapidly throughout the country. There seemed to be renewed interest in the always popular feel-good story in the magazines, newspapers, or on television. Was there a driving force to open all records? Somehow that did not sound fair or compassionate to everyone involved.

Predictably, the story coverage always showed happy reunions between a birth parent and a usually grown, adult adoptee with the smiling adoptive family members distantly included in the background. But was a "reunion" always that way, warm and welcoming, friendly and forgiving? Many people privately wondered.

The real-life version of having a child out of wedlock was not a warm and fuzzy story—which many media outlets loved to ignore in their cover story. The pregnancy itself covered nine months of emotional ups and downs, potentially a great deal of physical pain, numerous medical appointments and restrictions, often loss of income, possible loss of friends or family connections, or isolation and loneliness. It could ruin a marriage as well when involving affairs, infidelity, divorces, or just breakups of relationships due to different priorities.

Abortion has always been an option for pregnancies, whether legal or illegal, even safe or unsafe, throughout the centuries and the whole world. A pregnant birth mother considering adoption makes a choice, a choice for life. She often does so in spite of all the hardship, in spite of the stigma placed on her by society, and in spite of all her own personal desires and plans.

In most societies and countries, a pregnant woman considering the choice of adoption has always been awarded privacy in some form or another and has crafted laws and contracts designed to protect her. The beginning of efforts to open that lockbox of protection was frightening for many people. There was an original agreement between parties and her choices and actions were based on promises made in honor and accepted. What right did others now have to tear up that agreement and expose her to everything all over again? Is it not the height of arrogance to second guess someone's actions and motives in a completely different time?

Courts, legislators, adoption organizations, and social services around the country continued to grapple with the issue, hoping for an easy solution for all parties but there was no easy solution. Every case was personal. Every case was different. And there was always a lot of emotion in every case: fear, anger, hope, resentment, frustration, guilt, and love in many different forms.

What would each party want from the other? Did they want a new family, to spend holidays together forever, meet for lunch once a year, to only share pictures, or provide financial support or repayment? I needed to decide what I wanted. In my case, that did not seem too hard to do. I did not want a new family. I only wanted to know, not really *why*, because that was truly her business. I wanted to know *who* she was and what she looked like, and most importantly to me, to tell her I was fine and to thank her.

The Cradle began to offer a service to adopted children and birth parents. For $450 per parent, they would search for them *for* adoptees. All I would have to do is wait. It made perfect sense because they knew everything there was to know, certainly more than I could dig up on my own. They had all the tools, all the magic to make it happen.

After their search, when they found the other person, the same rules of engagement would apply as before, required counseling sessions of both parties separately and then eventually, supervised meetings together. I mailed the fee off the next day, more hopeful than I had been in a long time during all my years of research work. I could almost relax.

The following week, I was delighted to already receive a response back from The Cradle including one of my checks for $450. They said that their records indicated my birth father had passed away in 1977, over twenty years before, and they would look for an obituary or relatives in the area in which he had lived and would not charge me for that limited search.

So, basically, they were telling me that my efforts over the decades as I searched for Elizabeth, who may have been my only possible link to my birth father, had always been pretty much hopeless. That link would have been to someone who was already dead, had been dead in fact, for darn near forever. So much for that parent. I was angry. It was certainly not The Cradle's fault, but it was frustrating to lose a race against time without even getting past a walking pace.

I was approaching fifty. The "system" had withheld information from me from the very first day and taken away any chance of knowing a birth father, shaking his hand, learning about his life, or hearing his voice, but I could win myself the booby prize of maybe finding an obituary.

I took whatever crumbs were left available to me and waited it out. In spite of my random requests for updates, it would be several years before there was any more concrete information from their search for the elusive Elizabeth.

And they never found any obituary for my birth father.

CHAPTER TWENTY-EIGHT

2001 was an earthquake of a year for nearly everyone. The events of September 11 affected us all in different ways. At that time in our lives, we already had a beautiful grandson and were again blessed with the arrival of our first granddaughter. My husband and I began a new business, a bed and breakfast inn inside a one-hundred-year-old Victorian house which took two years of renovation—while my husband still continued his day job. Our parents also required our help in many different ways.

To put it mildly, there was a lot going on in our lives and I was so busy that I almost forgot about The Cradle's searches. I knew they were "working on them" but they never seemed to produce any answers. Having done a lot of searching myself, I knew their efforts might not pay off easily since it had been nearly fifty years and could even be hopeless at this point. No doubt they were also trying to help many people besides me.

I had been completely out of search ideas for a good while and hardly had a minute to think about it even if one had popped into my head. Then, one day out of the blue, I received a letter from The Cradle. It read:

"Dear Ms. Guillotte:

I am writing regarding the searches we are conducting for your birth family members. I realize that these searches have been on-going for quite some time. I imagine that this time has probably been frustrating and depressing.

If that is accurate, my feelings are similar to yours regarding these searches. In the search for your birth mother, we did find that she is deceased. This was difficult to determine because of the different names she used and different spellings that were used of her names. The name under which she died, Bette Ryan, does not appear in our records. We have had confirmation from Social Security that this is the person known to us as your birth mother. Unfortunately, your birth mother's life seems to have continued to be quite difficult. According to the death certificate she took her own life."

I stopped reading. I remember thinking, *Oh my God* as if someone put a stun gun to my body. I could not think any further for a few moments and stared blankly into the air in our small home office, not hearing or really seeing or feeling anything yet, just a numbness to movement and thought. After some time, I continued reading the letter:

"The circumstances of your birth mother's death did not give us much hope in being able to locate her daughter, your birth sister. We have utilized hundreds of hours of search time and every search data base known to us, our search consultant, and the state sponsored search service. We have not been able to locate any information regarding your birth sister."

She continued:

"I have talked with our legal consultant regarding the unusual circumstances of your search. Based on his legal opinion and our clinical practice, I am able to share with you the death certificate we received for your birth mother. Generally we are not able to share this document without permission from the next of kin. Since we are not able to locate the next of kin, and since we feel strongly that you deserve to have some documentation to assist in your closure and grief, I can share this with you. I am not enclosing it in this letter only because I wanted you to have an opportunity to let this sink in. When you are ready to receive it I will send it to you.

You had also requested that we attempt to contact your birth father. Because we had such little information about him, I did not cash your check upon receipt of it two years ago. I have tried to find information about him but have not been successful. I had found an entry in the Social Security Death Index that seemed to match his name and general year of birth, but I've not been able to secure any verification of his death. Letters to people with the same last name in the area where your birth mother reported he was from have not been successful in reaching anyone who can assist in locating his family.

I regret that the outcome of your Search is not a positive one. Some people have told me that while their search outcome was disappointing, they also felt closure in recognizing that they had done everything they could do to try to locate their birth family.

I realize that it may take some time for this to be real. If you would like to talk or if you have questions please don't hesitate to contact me. I can be reached at (123)-456-7890 or by my email.

Sincerely,

MG"

How could this happen? How could she have done that? Could I have helped or stopped her? Where was her family? Why? How? I never saw that coming. I had no clear familiar knowledge of suicide.

Several years before, one of my coworkers lost his only son to suicide, devastating him and their family members. Normally the jokester of the office, we had never seen him so broken in spirit. After the funeral, his only comment to me was, "Everything is fixable, except suicide." I knew now more than ever what that meant. It was final.

All those things I could have told her, all those questions I might have asked her, all those things I could have noticed were similarities, disappeared instantly as if they were never real anyway. And why?

CHAPTER TWENTY-NINE

My husband traveled constantly in his day job and was rarely available for talking while away. I left a message on his cell phone not knowing where he was or when he would be able to call me back. I tried to sound calm in my voice and wording. I had to tell him about the letter, but who else would I or could I be able to tell?

I got in the car and drove to Mom's house. My dad had passed away two years before and Mom had an active life with many friends, but this afternoon, thankfully, she was home. She could tell by the look on my face as soon as I walked into her kitchen. She hugged me silently and we sat at the table. I did not need to find the words. I gave her the letter and watched her patiently read through it to the end. She consoled me as only a mother can, mothers who cannot stand to see their child in pain—although she felt helpless to lessen its reality.

It took me a couple of weeks to call Maureen, at The Cradle. I was not particularly religious in my walk-through life. Raised by a Methodist/Baptist mom, we attended the Methodist church in town until the ladies of the church complained to Mom that she was not volunteering enough of her time. Her response was to give them exactly no more of her inadequate amount of time and we promptly switched to the Episcopal Church down the street.

Dad had taken a course in Theology and Religious Studies in college and decided he liked Mary Baker Eddy's writings as the basis of the Christian Scientist theories. Like many husbands, to keep peace in the house, he was happy to follow Mom's lead when it came to churchgoing. He and Mom both felt that the most important point was to provide their child with some religious instruction as a guide for life and that I could choose my own way later on, as an adult.

I accepted the Episcopal Church's teachings, the Bible, and loved growing up in the Episcopal Church, going to chapel every morning at school. Later in life, my participation dwindled for otherworldly reasons but not because I lost faith or belief. Under those teachings, I felt that suicide was a sin, but I also fully understood that all of us humans fail in attempts to achieve any goals near perfection. I had no idea what could have made her think that suicide was to be her best or only answer. At this time, I had no knowledge of how dark her heart had felt or what might be her sad reasoning.

When it felt like the right time, I took some quiet time in the home office and dialed the number to The Cradle. Maureen took my call right away and her voice was as warm and compassionate as I anticipated from her letter. I did not really know what to say even though hundreds of words were going through my thoughts. Thankfully, she started our conversation.

"Susan, I am so glad you called. This is an excellent time for me to talk and I am at your disposal, as they say. I am sure you have many questions and emotions," she offered, as if I was the only baby in one hundred years that The Cradle had to worry about. I felt a tinge of guilt at the past feelings of resentment towards The Cradle when I was young. Absolutely none of this situation was their fault and they always had my best interest at heart.

"I do. I just don't know how to start." After I got going, I told her how frustrated I was that my search had ended in this. She totally understood my frustration and feelings, but it could not change the situation as it existed. It reminded me of one of my daughter's favorite expressions, "It is what it is," and indeed, it was. Eventually, she asked, "I have your file in front of me. Do you feel you are ready for me to send you the death certificate?"

I swallowed and breathed. "Yes, I guess I'm ready."

"Do you have any questions about it before we mail it? I will answer any question at all that I can."

The words just flowed out of my brain, almost involuntarily, "Are you sure it is her? It's a very common name. How can you know for sure?"

"Unfortunately, we are certain. This case has been the most difficult one in all our searches. As you know it has taken many years. The Cradle hired a private investigator to trace your birth mother's names and locations. He spent hours on the case, following up all along the way.

"We confirmed it with Social Security as well. By doing that, we were also able to get a copy of her original application for a Social Security number. The copy shows her original name and her Social Security number, which we are also going to send you. With that information, you will be more informed. That additional information should enable you to do your own research in greater depth going forward."

I had to say it. "Do you know how she committed suicide?"

Maureen spoke softly and slowly, "Yes, it was a gunshot to her head." It felt like a slap. All I could do was breathe. I did not know what to say next. For some reason, a picture of the guns in my parents' house came to mind. Dad had two prized possessions, his shotgun and his 22 which he always took hunting. They hung on our den wall on a wooden rack. I never had any fear of guns growing up. This was not about the gun but the person.

"I am so sorry about this, Susan. I will put all this in the mail to you. I am sure you will have more questions later on. Any time you think of one, please call me. I can talk to you any time. Are you okay?"

"I am. I'm okay. It is just so sad. It just closes all the doors." I paused and Maureen did not speak. "Thank you for all your work on it," I told her earnestly from my heart. I wanted her to understand how much I appreciated everything they had done for my situation. No doubt it was not easy for them either and they never gave up on me.

In a few days, I received the documents in the mail from The Cradle. The death certificate was from the state of California and the city was San Francisco. There it was in black and white, cause of death: "Penetrating Contact Gunshot Wound to the Head." I quickly started to scan the other information but stopped, telling myself I needed to read it from the top. What was the hurry if she was already gone?

A lot of information was either missing or typed "unknown" in the blanks. Her name was Betty Ryan, apparently a married name, new to me. The coroner did not even know her date of birth, place of birth, Social Security number, or age; he estimated her age as 50+. The date of her death was August 5, 1983.

I knew nothing about San Francisco, having only visited there for a few days of vacation coincidentally around that time. Her death took place at 957 Mission Street, #129, in San Francisco, which I assumed was an apartment building. I wondered if I had been anywhere near that area when on vacation. We had seen Lombard Street, the docks, the sea lions, and rode a trolley car, enjoying all the beauty of the city's tourist highlights. Now it felt bizarre to even remember those happy moments.

Her body was never claimed, and it was cremated thirty days later by a mortuary under contract with the city or state to handle unclaimed persons. Why was there no family and so little information included? It said her ashes were then buried at sea. I remembered seeing the beautiful seacoast around Monterey and felt a wisp of comfort thinking she was in a place many people probably called heaven on earth for its beauty.

One question stood out so boldly after reading the entire form that my mind still discounted its evidentiary value. I could not feel the connection to the certificate, the blank spaces, the event, or that deceased person yet. How could they decide that this was indeed my Elizabeth Cobb or my actual birth mother? If this was my proof, I could not see it. Where was Mr. Ryan if she had been married at some time? Why California? What happened to Chicago? Where was an explanation for all my questions? Who could tell me now if this piece of paper was all there was left of her?

The other form from The Cradle was the "Application for Social Security Account Number." Indeed, that had some surprising information. Not only was her Social Security number handwritten by someone at the top of the form, but most importantly, it gave her full name from birth, Betty Isabella Benson. That would be a starting point for me instead of the Elizabeth Cobb that had gone nowhere.

I began to call her "Betty." The photocopy of the application form also gave me her date of birth, place of birth, her personal signature at the bottom, and her parents' full names. It opened up yet another state, being born in Alabama, broadening the search area yet again. I had a lot of work to do to travel into Betty's world.

CHAPTER THIRTY

Fortunately for me, I now had a new search buddy. After reading the letter informing me of the suicide, Mom dove into the internet with our small basket of new clues. She spent hours emailing and looking up names and addresses online. Her computer was on a desk in her kitchen, and it was piled with printouts and surrounded by sticky notes.

Mom made great progress and found Betty's parents' background information, including lots of newspaper articles. Mom printed out reams of copies of data and email conversations. She joined Ancestry. com just to search for me and emailed people all over the country asking questions.

Betty's father, my grandfather, had been a farmer in southern Alabama. His parents were from Michigan, and they all came down to the lower coastal country of Alabama when he was a young man. They had a large family farm called Riverglimpse Farm in Summerdale and were well respected in the area. He married my grandmother, Betty's mother, in 1922. She was named Marguerite and nicknamed "Maggie." They had Betty in 1923 and she was their only child.

The Cradle had relayed to me that Betty told them her father "died in an auto accident." I wondered about playing the old children's post office game when a sentence is whispered around a circle of children to see how well it survives details and meaning passed from ear to ear. It is hard to determine if Betty told them incorrectly, if they recorded the information incorrectly, or just relayed it to me incorrectly.

Regardless of the cause of the discrepancy, we discovered that he did not actually die from an auto accident at all. There was much more to the story as found in a local Alabama newspaper article's account of his death. He was only forty-two years old.

The *Fairhope Courier* newspaper wrote:

Paul T. Benson, whose tragic death was noted in last week's issue, was buried last Thursday with Rev. Jordan officiating and the American Legion in charge of the grave.

The *Courier* is furnished by a member of the family the following fuller particulars as to how he met his death.

"His sad departure from this life was an outcome of his generous nature to help others whenever possible. A friend running low on gasoline stopped to borrow some, and returning it, left the gasoline can while no one was home. In lighting a fire [in his home] Mr. Benson picked up the gasoline can, believing it to be kerosene and poured it on the fire which caused an explosion burning him severely. He put out his burning clothing: the house having caught, he put that fire out, gave himself first aid, put on scant clothing, then made an effort to crank his car which he could not do on account of the burned hands; then walked a quarter mile to the nearest neighbor and called them to bring their car and carry him to a doctor."

"Mr. Benson was a native of Michigan, born at St. Joseph, and lived a good part of his early years at Berrien Springs, and Niles, where he met his wife, a Chicago girl.

He studied banking and law at the American Institute of Banking and was connected with the First National Bank of Detroit. He served overseas during the World War, afterwards coming south to live.

Mr. Benson was well-known and liked in this vicinity."

It was heartbreaking to read the reports. Tragic just did not seem to be a big enough word for it but then, what word would be? Anyone who has ever had a small burn knows the size of that pain. It was inconceivable to me how much pain he must have endured but I hoped he had been given a lot of drugs to sleep. More and more information, and again, it was yet another death.

Thankfully through the blessings of small-town newspapers and the people who were smart enough to save them, there was a great deal of information on the Benson couple.

The society pages told me where they went to dinner with friends, at Dr. Manick's farm or others, and when my grandmother entertained guests or went to Chicago to visit her family. The classified ads told me when they needed extra help on the farm or wanted to sell or buy farm equipment. "Strawberry Plants for Sale" ads told me what they produced on their farm. My grandfather was active in the Baldwin County politics and well respected from those reports.

By law, the federal government conducts a national census every ten years. The collected information is not released to the public for seventy-two years. Each decade's census records a great deal of data on each person which can be a gold mine for ancestry research.

After her husband's death, my grandmother, Maggie, had an eleven-year-old daughter, which was not an easy situation for a woman in 1934. She left the farm and moved to nearby Mobile. According to the 1940 Census, they had income other than employment wages, probably from the farm revenue.

Very strangely, there were no school records anywhere showing Betty ever went to school at all covering Alabama, nearby states, or even in Illinois. She was physically there in Mobile with her mother for the 1940 Census and it stated she had completed four years of high school. She was not working.

At the time of that census collection, around April of 1940, she was seventeen years old. Incredibly, I was never able to find any record of her after that single point in time. It would be several years later before the 1950 Census would be released to the public. Maggie, my grandmother, did work while in Mobile as a secretary, an editor, and even as a musician until the early 1940s and she addressed herself simply as Margaret Benson in those employment records.

CHAPTER THIRTY-ONE

At some point, I needed to get back to the basics of researching my immediate birth parents rather than just my grandparents. Knowing the Benson name and locations made it easy to see their ancestral line all the way back into the 1600s. I could see that they came to America from Germany and discovered a very strong British background as well.

Having the information from Maureen at The Cradle provided lots of tools but like all adoption searches, you simply had to keep digging and Mom was basically using a backhoe all over the internet. With the discovery of the suicide and Mom's very active pursuits, I basically dropped my own shovel. How much dirt did I honestly want to dig up, literally? In my mind, I knew what step was necessary to go forward but my heart dreaded it.

I talked to my husband, an ex-police officer, about the records that San Francisco may have kept on the suicide, half hoping he might say they likely purged them after some arbitrary number of years. He said I would only know if I asked. My mom could see I was fearful of more bad news but, truly, we already knew it was bad. One of her favorite movies was "Annie," and especially the version starring Albert Finney and Carol Burnette. She quoted Punjab's words from the movie, "A child without courage is like a night without stars."

I finally mustered the courage and called California. It took a couple of days to connect through all the San Francisco Police Department offices, and find the right person, who then needed to locate the old file and call me back when we both had the time to talk. All that was in addition to dealing with the time differences from coast to coast.

The homicide detective who took my original call was another one of those gifts along the way through our search. I wondered if he regretted answering the phone and having to deal with my request, but if that were true, it never showed.

He seemed energetic in his response, and I felt like a great deal of patience and understanding was in his voice. His actions proved that to be true when we were finally able to settle down with the file and discuss it over the phone. His voice was so kind and slow and compassionate. I will call him Lieutenant H.

With the whole file in front of him, he said, "Are you ready for this stuff, kiddo? I don't want to upset you."

I took a deep breath and said, "I know it's not pretty, but I think I am ready," and then he gave me a shock I never saw coming.

"Ok, you know it was a murder-suicide, right?" and I gasped. No, I did not know that. I did now. Not only had she taken her own life, but she killed somebody else, too. This was getting totally out of hand, out of my limits of comprehension. Where was the end to the bad news and heartbreaking shocks? How could I possibly make any sense out of this?

Lieutenant H. summarized the information in the file. He continued to speak slowly and softly, asking me repeatedly if I was "still okay, kiddo?" It is amazing to me that police officers dedicate their careers and often their whole lives to constantly dealing with such horrific crimes and situations. The rest of us think a bad day at the office is when the copier breaks down.

Lieutenant H. gradually revealed the story. In San Francisco, Betty lived with her son, Johnny, in a hotel for welfare recipients, a form of subsidized housing. They had lived there for three years. From the reports of the hotel manager, Johnny was disabled in some way, and abusive to his mother, Betty. He would beat her if she refused to buy him wine. They had basically no belongings in the sparsely furnished apartment.

From the police reports on the scene, the hotel manager checked on the apartment because Betty had not come down to the office to get her milk delivery. The manager found them on the floor of their living room at about 1:00 p.m. and called the police.

Betty had wrapped Johnny in a blanket, shot him in the back of his head, and then shot herself in the head. She left a suicide note, written on the back of a month-old notice from the hotel management about upcoming plumbing repairs to the building. Lieutenant H. asked me again if I was okay. I could barely respond with a yes. I was speechless and the tears were silently dropping onto my lap as the detective read me the note she had left to the world. It read, exactly:

"My son Alan is the kindest sweetest boy there ever was and smart. Children and animals loved him. He always did whatever he could to help me and others. He helped me <u>many</u> times. If I had of listened to him in the first place, we never would have ended up in San Francisco. I cost him his home four years ago and his money just by leaving for a while to get medicine and vitamins. At least it ended up that way. It is too long a story. Jean [hotel manager], the sleeping bag blanket you brought us up from the basement June 6th, 1980 was full of lice. It even got in my shoes right off. We fought it and fought. I could never try on the clothes. It got all over us. Ate my feet up. Been in terrible pain all the time here. He had perfect teeth when he came here. – I would have done this before but could not get the G___ till this morning. We used to be two happy people. Everyone loved him."

He read me all the information from the police and coroner's reports. The physical description sounded like it could be Betty, but was it? There were no social security numbers or other identifying info at all on either person. The police file included copies of their hotel application that listed only their names. And who in the world was Johnny? If Johnny was his name on the hotel records, why did she refer to him as "Alan" in her note?

There were several photos in the file, photos from the crime scene and the autopsy. Lieutenant H said, "You really do not want to see them and they would not tell you much anyway." I knew he was right. Even if I was sitting there with him, I don't think I could bring myself to look at the crime scene photos.

At the conclusion of our phone call, he offered to send me copies of everything in the file except the photos. When I received the package the following week, I found included in the paperwork, a copy of a newspaper article from the San Francisco Examiner. It read:

Stuffed animals only witnesses to their deaths
By Beth Hughes
Examiner Staff Writer
Only some stuffed animals witnessed the shootings, a possible mur-

der-suicide in a sparsely furnished South of Market apartment occupied by a middle-aged woman and her disabled adult son.

"We have no idea what caused this," homicide inspector Earl Sanders said. "Their circumstances were shockingly depressing."

Police arrived at 957 Mission St. about 1:15 p.m. Friday to find two bodies in a "very, very, very sparsely furnished" apartment, homicide inspector Napoleon Hendrix said.

Some stuffed animals "that a child would have" provided the only decoration, police said.

The two had lived in the apartment for three years, Sanders said, and their income came from public assistance benefits.

Witnesses told police the man was physically and mentally disabled.

Police are investigating the possibility that the woman shot her son with a "small-caliber handgun, a derringer," and then shot herself, Sanders said.

The victims' names were being withheld pending notification of their family.

End of article

* * *

As adopted children, we have all kinds of different experiences that non-adopted children would never even think about. We can look at other families and instantly see the similarities in their looks, voices, and sometimes behaviors. Everyone in my adopted family had blue eyes and mine were greenish hazel. I was much taller than my mom and dad. Sometimes, only the differences stand out.

Medical family histories can be very valuable information in some lines of people for many diseases such as cancers, diabetes, heart problems, or arthritis. My ordinary visits to any doctor required the usual forms to complete about my family history. That was easy for me. I always wrote, "No family history, adopted." Now I could almost laugh about an answer such as, "Nothing but suicide so far." Of course, I never used it. But I was beginning to wonder how much of the tragedy I had found so far was actually in me, too. It was hard to not wonder now about myself.

CHAPTER THIRTY-TWO

Acceptance is often a slow, gradual process, requiring different steps for the heart and mind. There was no doubt that the murder-suicide happened but connecting *that* Betty Ryan to me was still unclear. Throughout this whole journey, it was difficult not to internalize the results. If this was really my birth mother, what was the risk that I could be like her?

Everyone experiences some degree of depression and anxiety in life. How deep would my natural genes go to drive my future? I was already a grandmother at this point. Had I dodged a miserable life by simply landing in a great family or could I still be affected by an unknown, unseen past?

I had felt low points in my life and experienced some episodes of depression. I assumed everyone did. Dad always said we should not skimp in life on three priorities: food, education, and medical. Not skimping did not mean overspending would be justifiable or acceptable. With his Christian Science belief as his basis, he was always a bit skeptical of throwing money or pills at a problem without a healthy amount of education and research. I looked into non-chemical help, which provided life skills for dealing with disappointments and life's anxieties. It required dedication and work, but it gave me the tools to approach problems with a healthy logic and appreciation for reality.

Over the next couple of years, I lost my mom, thereby losing my search buddy and best friend. We lost my husband's mom and dad as well. Changes were in the works. We were selling our bed and breakfast and making the "downsizing" move to a smaller house in the country. It was our long-term goal. We had both enjoyed growing up in the country and wanted to go back, especially to give our city grandchildren a taste of country life while still young.

As usual, it felt like there was a lot going on, but my good friend from childhood suggested strongly that I try the popular DNA test through Ancestry.com. I promised I would think about it. Rather than unpack what seemed like a million boxes after moving, I finally decided to try the test.

I do not want to sound like a commercial for these companies who provide the tests and website access, but I have to relate my own experience if I'm going to continue telling this story. For me, it was like entering a giant room of my own personal life and information, as if data could have arrived in a treasure chest.

On the website, my DNA test matched me to other DNA matches. It listed them by their closest proximity to my test results such as my first or second cousin. To my shock, I actually had a real cousin—alive! It was a man's name, and he was a "first" cousin. I'll call him Page.

I never paid much attention to the designation of first or second cousins or the terminology of "once removed." Mom had a big family. I had several cousins and I just thought of them all as my cousins, my family. But this position of "first" cousin was meaningful in the DNA status line and I needed to learn what it was.

It gets a little tangled up here, at least it did for me anyway. I really needed to think about it all with total concentration. It may sound childish but drawing stick figure diagrams helped me to keep it straight in my head. In the diagram shown here, I started at the bottom showing "ME" and "Page" and then moved upwards to our parents.

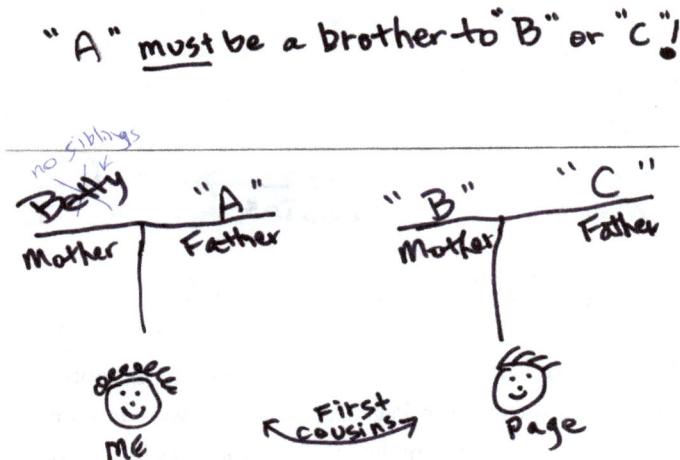

" A " must be a brother to "B" or "C"!

no siblings

Betty — "A"   "B" — "C"
Mother | Father   Mother | Father

ME   First cousins   Page

If Page was a first cousin to me, then our parents had to somehow be sisters, or brothers, or sister and brother. I could eliminate Betty because she was an only child and had no siblings. With that in mind, Page's mom (B) or dad (C) *had* to be a brother or sister to *my* dad (A). Could this be that easy? All I had to do was keep it straight in my brain. My brain was definitely not that reliable. I had to constantly refer to these pictures.

The ancestry site offered a way for me to message anyone listed as my other DNA matches. I wrote a note to Page and was excited to hear back right away. The answer came from Page's wife. He was a very busy guy, and she was responding for him.

It turned out that Page knew who his mother was, but he did not know his father. His mother had unfortunately passed away and would never tell him who his father had been, in spite of his requests to understand.

Page's mother had one sister, but she did not have any brothers. They were hopeful that if I could find my father (A), it might tell Page who his father was (C). They had to be brothers. I had no clue how to find my father yet, but I promised I would let them know if I did. I also had to draw a new picture to keep this growing world organized.

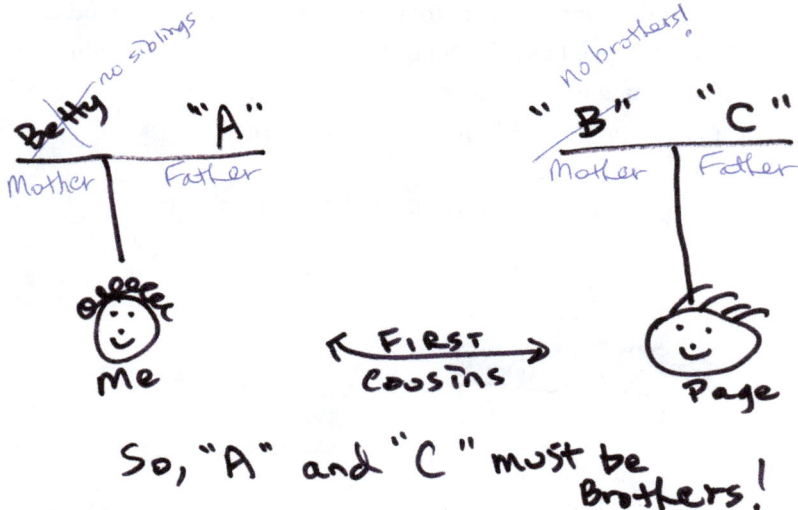

While that pot was simmering on one burner, I got another message on the site, but it wasn't from Page. It was from a woman named Karen. She was much further down my list of DNA matches in relation to me, a fourth to sixth cousin. I was amazed that the numbers could go that high. This was really going to get confusing. I would need lots of stick figures and flow charts to keep anything straight.

Karen was very experienced in genealogy. She determined we had grandmothers who had the same names and that they were cousins. My grandmother was Marguerite Marie Wollweber (Betty's mother) and co-incidentally, that was also her grandmother's name but by marriage; her grandmother married my grandmother's brother. They had nicknames to keep them straight. My grandmother was Maggie, and her grandmother was Rhea. So, with the introduction of Karen, I had another relative and as it turned out, a very nice friend.

Not only was Karen kind enough to reach out to me as a new member on the site, but she proved to be a wealth of knowledge. Her cousin Susan had a very large collection of family genealogical records spanning decades and even centuries. It was all on Betty's mother's side, the Wollweber's side. She offered to check with Susan about my specific direction of family research, Maggie's daughter Betty.

Karen and her cousin Susan were so generous to me, putting together a large packet of copies of documentation. Several pages showed the history and stories of that side of my family. I actually saw a picture of Maggie's mother, father, and siblings—which would be my great grandparents, great aunts, and great uncles. I had to laugh when I saw a picture of one of the great uncles. It showed a startling resemblance to my grandson. Even if they were all long since deceased, for once, this felt like good news, and it was fun to read all the stories about their lives.

I thanked Karen and Susan heartily for all the information. Their generosity would come to be a shining first example of so many people involved in family and genealogical research, often strangers who are willing to provide family details, give advice, and share ideas in your journey. Certainly, there are privacy risks to consider, and caution for safety's sake should always be a searcher's guiding rule, but I was often overwhelmed by their interest and willingness to help whenever they could. They even helped to search with me.

CHAPTER THIRTY-THREE

The website Ancestry.com opened up a huge world of searchable data for me unlike anywhere else, all in one place. I could search names in a hundred different ways, adding or limiting filters endlessly. I could lose hours of time reading documentation, legal records, reading family trees, and viewing pictures.

The toughest part was always trying to figure out if the Betty online was *my* Betty, especially with millions of people with a last name of Benson or even Ryan. Again, I wished her last name was something crazy with about twenty letters! Was I getting somewhere or just spinning my wheels? It was often hard to tell the difference.

With that in mind, I decided to focus on my grandmother's side of the family, hoping it would give me more information on that elusive Betty, who disappeared at the age of seventeen in 1940. She didn't physically disappear, of course. She was definitely somewhere between 1940 and 1983 if she actually died in 1983. I just could not find the first concrete record anywhere. With the size of this country, information could just about be anywhere.

I learned from Karen that the Wollweber name was often spelled Wallweber. Apparently, there was a very famous spy during World War II named Wollweber, and many family members wished to change their name spelling to avoid any connection to that unrelated traitor. With the way my family tree was developing, I was just glad that the Wollweber spy was not related to me. Just what I needed to add to my not-so-illustrious growing family tree, a national traitor, too.

Through the online site, I found my grandmother Maggie's death certificate. Although married in Alabama, she died in California in 1969, yet another connection to a state I really knew very little about. She was still a Benson, never having gotten remarried. I sent away for a copy of the death certificate and filed it away in my Maggie pile. Keeping everything organized was always a challenge. Everyone had a "pile" with their first name.

Having fairly exhausted the Wollweber line, I turned back to two other searches, finding my father and finding my half-sister. I hope the reader will not need Dramamine while reading this. I apologize for bouncing all over the subjects, but it accurately portrays the way these searches happen in real life. Most of the time, a search reveals a piece of information—like finding Maggie's death certificate online—but then there is the delay until it comes in the mail which often takes weeks. So, onward, to another direction in the meantime.

I had no name for my half-sister, and Betty's information was either nonexistent or too vague, no matter where I looked. Consequently, I focused on finding my father through the only two clues I thought were available: the biological connection to Page, somehow, assuming our fathers were brothers, and the fact that my father had supposedly worked for the post office as a supervisor, according to The Cradle. If I could find my father, surely it would solve Page's mystery too.

There is a registry database available online of all the postmasters in the history of this country. The creation of the United States Post Office dates back to 1775, and the position of postmaster began in 1780. Estimating by my date of birth, I scanned the dates and names for something that might be a possibility. No luck. The United States Postal Service is such a large organization. My needle in that haystack could really be anywhere in the country.

I switched to what I knew about Page. His wife and I corresponded, and she provided as much information as possible. A phone call with both of them filled in the rest of what they knew so far. Ironically, Page was born an hour away from where I now live. We were a year apart in age and he had grown up close by where I grew up. Could that city, Richmond, Virginia, be a clue as well? If our fathers were brothers, the proximity of our childhoods in the state of Virginia was an amazing thought.

I spent a lot of time doing a million searches for people Page knew about, starting with his biological mother, Phyllis. She was already deceased. Before she passed away, Page had been allowed to contact her through the State of Virginia adoption agency.

Phyllis went to her grave with her secret, never confessing who Page's father was. Throughout her life, she had three children with three different men, two of whom she was married to, so those men were known and searchable. However, neither of those searches produced any helpful results to solve the mystery for Page and me.

Page was the middle child and Phyllis had given him up for adoption in Richmond. Did that mean his birth father was nearby also, possibly still in the Richmond area? It was impossible to guess at this point, but it could be considered as very likely.

It is a curiosity to observe people's living patterns, often not traveling very far from their birthplace during their lives. In spite of the fact that The Cradle had told me that my biological father was deceased, I could find out a lot more about his life if it had taken place so close by to my current home in Virginia. My husband was a Virginia boy, was born in Richmond, and knew the area far better than I did. There is a saying in Virginia, that "all roads lead to Richmond."

I concentrated on Phyllis's family members, such as her mother and father and her grandparents, all readily available online with marriage certificates, birth records, and death certificates. Tracking her life could have told us where she may have met up with Page's birth father since I knew Page's date of birth. The online records showed that Phyllis's parents had several children, about seven all total, but only three survived childbirth and childhood. Three? But how could that be right? Page and his wife clearly said his mother had only one sister and no brothers.

From birth records online, I easily found that Phyllis indeed had an older brother. Apparently, she simply never mentioned it to Page in their communications. He was quite a bit older than Phyllis and he was the first-born child.

All of a sudden, the lightbulb lit up in my brain. That man, Phyllis's older brother, had to be my father. It made perfect sense. How else could Page and I be first cousins? Unless there were more people floating around that we did not know about, this was the only answer, and his name was Preston.

I could not wait to tell Page and his wife and called them right away. It was a great discovery for me, placing a name on my biological father, but unfortunately, it did not really help Page. We had assumed our fathers were brothers but that was clearly not the case. We were still indeed first cousins because his mother Phyllis and my father Preston were simply sister and brother.

Page and his wife were very happy for me in my discovery but no doubt disappointed that it did not give Page an answer yet. Like most discoveries in these pursuits, it had a silver lining, which was to force Page to look in a different direction.

Happily for him, that information opened a door soon after leading to discovering his father's information and finding a new sister. They spoke on the phone and were able to meet in person. I cannot take credit for really helping him solve his mystery, but it all feels like part of a giant puzzle. Sometimes we just have to move the pieces around some more.

CHAPTER THIRTY-FOUR

Finally, I now had a name, a full name, for my biological father. As The Cradle had told me, it was a very common name, but there was plenty of data on him with his unusual first name, Preston. I found where he was born, saw his draft card, read when he went into WWII and came home, and that he retired from the Rock Island Railroad, having worked for the post office for twenty-two years after the war.

How do you work for the post office and retire from a railroad? Which was it? At the time I was investigating all this, I coincidentally began working for the post office as well. Or was it a coincidence at all?

When I was younger, I wanted to work for the post office. The whole organization fascinated me, delivering all that giant volume of mail every day. It had been in place since about 1780. Benjamin Franklin was our country's first postmaster general. It has been copied by every country on our planet.

I know people like to make jokes about the post office and we have all had something get lost or delayed in transit. But to me, it always seemed like a miracle that a person could mail one letter in their mailbox and another person, perhaps living a thousand miles away could receive it in a few days, out of billions and billions of pieces of mail. Certainly, it wasn't a religious miracle but what kind of system could make that happen at all? Like I said, fascinating.

Unfortunately, I have lousy feet for running or for lots of walking. It never occurred to me that I could do something other than be a walking letter carrier when I was younger. Consequently, I dropped the idea and pursued other careers and passions.

When my husband and I downsized to our small town in the country, the local postmaster was looking for someone to hire, a clerk to cover her on a part-time basis, starting with every Saturday morning. It was a bit late in life, but I was excited about my new "career." I jumped at the chance to be her clerk; I would be living the dream.

With a small amount of study into post office history, I learned about RPOs. For over a century, beginning around the Civil War era, the United States Postal Service carried, delivered, and sorted mail on trains in cars which were called Railway Post Offices. They covered hundreds of routes through the whole continental United States. The

A very elite group of clerks operated on the RPOs. The job required memorizing complicated grids of train routes, lists of town names, time schedules of constant pickups and drop-off points, and mountains of rules and regulations. The men were rigorously tested on a constant basis, and they could be let go if they received a score of less than 95% or failed to sort the mail in time from one town to another—something they called "getting stuck."

The RPO career was recognized as a grueling occupation, standing on a moving train for ten or more hours, sorting mail constantly, often in frigid cold temperatures or roasting heat. The men had to be able to "catch" a hanging mailbag which would hang on a pole next to the railroad track while the train only slowed down a little. Clerks could lose their arms or even their lives in some cases.

The trains were all subject to fatal wrecks. Armed robberies by gangsters and ordinary thieves were common occurrences. All the clerks were issued side arms and ammunition by the Department of the Post Office to protect the mail and the crews in cases of attempted robbery. Each clerk was responsible for the care and maintenance of their firearm. The cars often carried huge sums of cash, coins, and bills, from one bank to another. An RPO was a tasty pick for robbing gangs.

Train travel was extensive throughout the country for decades and an RPO would go everywhere a train delivered passengers or just cargo. Well before the beginning of air travel, there were thousands of RPOs crisscrossing the countryside every day, normally located right behind the train engine and followed by a variety of passenger and freight cars. There was a letter slot on the outside of the train car which allowed any person to mail a letter like an ordinary mailbox on the street.

I was fortunate to access the railroad personnel records fairly easily.

The National Archives provided the information willingly when I inquired. Preston's career was based in Chicago on the Rock Island Railroad or the "Rock" as it was affectionately nicknamed. The Rock came out of the I.C., the gigantic Illinois Central Railway station.

Preston was born in Petersburg, Virginia. He died in Virginia six years after I graduated from high school and three years after my daughter was born. I grew up an hour away from him. I could have met him. I could have known him, but we never had the chance. At least I now knew this answer and maybe I could find out more online. What I did not expect to find was another cousin, right in Richmond.

Preston had two younger sisters, one being Phyllis, Page's mother, who had passed away, and another being Margaret. Great, that was yet another "Margaret" and even I was getting confused. I searched for her information and saw that she had children too, a daughter named Catherine. I kept looking.

I saw that Catherine got married at some point and I searched around under her married name. There was no death certificate so maybe she was still alive. It also showed "City Directory" information online. Hundreds of phone books were available online and it gave her phone number from a few years before. What the heck, I thought. I had been hung up on plenty of times. What's one more? I tried the number, and a woman actually answered the phone!

Amazingly, Catherine talked to me in spite of my sputtering out an explanation for the call and how I found her number. She is about ten years older than me and a wonderful person. I guess you can imagine how relieved I was at some good news. Currently, she is a delightful friend, and we talk often.

Catherine was able to tell me stories of her memories as a child being around Preston, her uncle. She even had two pictures of him. One was a picture of him in his late thirties with his two younger grown sisters, Margaret and Phyllis. It was hard to see much detail as the photo was taken several feet in front of the three of them.

The other picture is a close-up of Preston at about eight, with his younger sister Margaret, who was about four years old. They are very dressed up for the photo. He is in a sailor suit and has a slight smirk on his face as if he is not very happy at all to be in that sailor suit or to have his picture taken with his younger sister.

When I showed the picture to a close friend, she could not help but laugh. Her comment was "Yes, I've seen that smirk more than a few times." She was right. I compared it to a portrait of myself around that age and admittedly, I had the same smirk, not happy at all to be in that itchy dress.

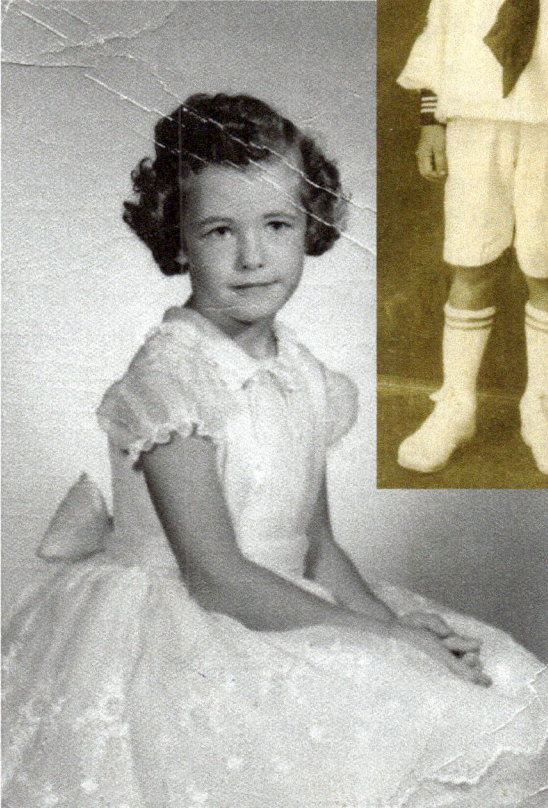

CHAPTER THIRTY-FIVE

As mentioned before in this writing, the help and support from fellow searchers online were invaluable. A casual discussion could reveal a huge clue at any moment. Their words of encouragement were like cookies to a hungry child in a long, drawn-out, never-ending childhood. It also helped to calm that nagging impatience; many people I encountered had been working on searches for many years as well.

Frustration was constant. Tedious recordkeeping was absolutely necessary. Even with the best organizing efforts, it was easy to lose your place after the smallest interruption. Recordkeeping required the "piles system," one pile for each person's data and documents, which took up a lot of office space and always looked like an untidy mess to everyone else.

Disappointment was often at the end of a trip into lengthy rabbit holes going nowhere, producing nothing but time lost and a large feeling of guilt that I could have done something much more productive over the afternoon. In those times, it was mentally helpful to walk away for sanity's sake and return to the table later, sometimes with no idea how to proceed.

One question continually nagged at me about the suicide and my connection to it. Betty's death certificate was supposedly verified by the Social Security Administration, but I could never trace Betty Ryan on the death certificate to me physically. Other than the Social Security bureaucracy saying so, I could not see the proof, especially with an adoption decree naming the completely invisible "Elizabeth Cobb."

Call me a big untrusting skeptic but I did not put a lot of faith in the average faceless federal employee who might have been in charge of matching up blank death certificates in their system to exact real people. Of course, I was clueless about how their system actually functioned, but my phone calls and questions about that mystery to various poor folks who took my calls at the Social Security offices did not provide any confidence or clear answers. They simply could not or would not explain how the process worked.

Social Security does have something called a Numident report which supposedly shows that connection—according to them, anyway. However, when I read Betty's Numident report, it was like Greek, or hieroglyphics, filled mostly with government codes. It also listed even more untraceable names, names I had never heard before.

I never found a marriage certificate for Betty Benson and any Mr. Ryan. Not all marriage records are online. They are held by each state individually and sometimes in each county. Not having a date, a location, or a first name for that Mr. Ryan made it fairly impossible to find. In addition, Betty Benson could have had another married name in that puzzle. It was getting muddy again and my boots were sticking in deep.

Perhaps somehow the proof would be in finding my half-sister if that could ever happen. I honestly felt very little hope. Family members questioned what good all the time was worth. They saw me struggling and honestly, it was an excellent question.

What could I even realistically hope to find at this point? That question was still impossible to answer out loud, but I questioned myself silently. How would I know what I wanted to find until I found it? But how long should I even try?

Karen, one of my fellow Ancestry.com searchers on Betty's side of my family said they did not have much at all in their family history on Betty. Nobody did, except for a date of birth. It was as if she died or vanished right after the 1940 Census—which simply showed her living in Mobile with her mother, Maggie. The Cradle had said there were "many name changes and locations" but I could not find anything. Was she changing her name on a whim? It certainly looked that way.

But one day, Karen found a record by one of her own relatives that said Betty had a child. It only had the first name. The child's name was Valerie, and she was nicknamed Bunny. I was completely stunned, speechless again. In a million years, I never would have dreamed of that coincidence.

Some people collect pigs, frogs, chickens, or dogs for fun and their houses may be full of their favorite characters. All my life, I had collected rabbits. I even had two live pet rabbits as a child. When very young, I was photographed often with a rabbit to induce me to smile.

When people find out you love rabbits, you often get them as gifts. I glanced around the room. I could see five in the first few seconds. Every room was like that. I actually felt a chill. Where in the world was this going? You might expect to have the same hair color as a relative, but a love for rabbits? That would be too much.

And now, having a first name for a half-sister, maybe I could actually find this Valerie before she died. I now called her by her nickname, Bunny.

I jumped in with both feet, searching every form of search parameters online. I was racing against an invisible clock that may have already run down because I knew she was much older than me. I tried every possible combination of her name and nickname. There were lots of answers out there but again, how could I tell which was the right answer, the right person? There were thousands of Valerie Ryan answers to pick from and no concrete way to narrow it down to the right one.

Tired of seemingly monotonous online roaming, I went back to the paper trails, leafing through piles of documents, notes, ideas, and even what I previously determined to be incorrect data. You keep everything because you never know when wrong data can become correct data overnight.

On top of my grandmother Maggie's pile sat her 1969 death certificate from California. This time, I read every line slowly. Most of the information had been meaningless when it first arrived. I had no connection to her home address in Palo Alto, California, or Maggie's occupation in Chicago. She had been a hotel manager.

Then I saw the "Informant" section on the death certificate. An informant is simply a person who calls the authorities to say the person has passed away and gives them the required facts needed for completion of the death certificate. Maggie's informant was a Mrs. Bunny Good who also lived at Maggie's address. Mrs. Bunny Good had to be Valerie. A nickname like Bunny was too big a coincidence. I now had a definite last name for Valerie.

I jumped back online and searched all over for a person named Bunny Good or Valerie Good. 99% of what came up was a newspaper comic strip about a cartoon character called Good Bunny. And there were 939 Valerie Good entries. I had to be patient and look through all of them, but I wasn't feeling patient at all. I needed to walk away again and start fresh the next day.

My house was filled with rabbits. We always joked about how they multiplied. Now they seemed to be a constant reminder of this new development. Would I get to meet her? I could fly to California. My mind and my heart were literally all over the map. In the days ahead, I tried to be methodical, taking one step at a time. I needed to check out all the Valerie Good entries online and try to eliminate all the wrong ones. I knew she was older than me, so I was able to filter the searches based on the range of birth years— but that only cut the number in half, still a huge group.

While messaging with Ruby, a fellow searcher online, I told her about my latest news and the huge sorting task ahead. She had always been so supportive and helpful through the years, and I had never even met her face to face. She was a crackerjack researcher, a nice friend to have on your side of the court. I hit a giant lob into the air by sharing this information and she caught the ball. She wrote back a cryptic note the next day and again, I never saw the ball coming right at me.

PART FIVE

California

CHAPTER THIRTY-SIX

I normally checked my Ancestry account daily, just to see if there were any new messages from people. Once in a blue moon, there would be a new distant cousin and I was usually tempted to check out their tree information for anything at all relevant to me.

This morning, there was a note from Ruby. She wrote "Susan, I think I may have found something that is extremely sad about Bunny. It may not be your half-sister but I'm just guessing that it is. I have attached the article I found in a Palo Alto newspaper. If you can't open it, I can send it by email. Take care and let me know what you think."

I immediately thought, *oh no, not more bad news*. What else can there be for bad news? I never would have dreamed in a million years that it could be the following article she sent to me published by the *Palo Alto News* Online:

NEWS

Longtime Palo Alto homeless woman dies at age 73.

'Bunny' Good died April 24, leaving a legacy of tenacity and sadness for those who tried to help

by Sue Dremann / Palo Alto Weekly

Uploaded: Wed, May 14, 2014, 1:44 pm 21

She wore a large 1940s wig -- Loretta Young-style -- and kept her face down. She took shelter under a blue plastic tarp with space for her two shopping carts. And when Valerie "Bunny" Good died on April 24, people who worked with her for decades grieved.

Good, 73, died of heart complications at Santa Clara Valley Medical Center after living on Palo Alto's streets for 34 years, said

Heiri Schupisser, homeless outreach specialist at the nonprofit Momentum for Mental Health in Palo Alto. On Monday afternoon, people attended a memorial service in her honor at All Saints Episcopal Church in Palo Alto.

Good was well known in Palo Alto, where she lived within a three-block area around University Avenue. She lived behind the old Apple store on the corner of University Avenue and Waverley Street and behind the 7-Eleven on Lytton Avenue, where a cinder block wall had provided her with privacy and protection from the wind. Most recently, she took up residence across from the University Avenue Starbucks, Schupisser said.

"I was surprised that she made it through the winter," Schupisser said.

He and others had tried for years to find appropriate housing for Good, but she was adamant there was only one place she wanted to live: senior housing community Lytton Gardens.

"She wanted to stay in Palo Alto. It was her home," Schupisser said.

Palo Alto police Chief Dennis Burns even wrote a letter to Lytton Gardens on her behalf, attesting that she was not a troublemaker. She didn't drink or use drugs, but she did suffer from depression, Schupisser said.

But she languished on a waiting list. Schupisser helped her receive Social Security benefits and straightened out a bank error that left her without payments for 3.5 years.

Good had been unhoused since December 1980. Toward the end of her life, she was finally willing to take other accommodations. She lived life the way she wanted to, and she wasn't willing to compromise, Schupisser said. That determination perhaps helped her to survive decades beyond the life expectancy for a homeless person, which is just seven years, he said.

Dr. Joel Wolfberg, a retired therapist who volunteers with Momentum for Mental Health in Palo Alto, worked to help Good. He visited her in the hospital before she died, and he remembers her fondly. In Wolfberg's opinion, she was also the victim of social and political indifference, he said last week.

Good's situation, living surrounded by Silicon Valley's riches, "is unconscionable to me," he said. "She didn't deserve to be raped in downtown Palo Alto or beaten up and made blind in one eye."

If Good seemed a shadowy figure to most passersby, she was to many "a remarkable woman," Schupisser said. She had a degree in mathematics from the University of Chicago; worked at Stanford Linear Accelerator (now SLAC National Accelerator Laboratory) in the 1960s, and at NASA Ames Research Center. When she left her job to take care of her grandmother, NASA wouldn't guarantee her a position when she returned. There was a divorce from her physicist husband and a mental breakdown, Wolfberg said.

But some people did look out for her. Palo Alto police officers often brought Good coffee in the morning, and Apple Store employees let her use the computers despite her poor hygiene, Schupisser said.

Her death is at least the second of an elderly homeless woman on Palo Alto's streets in five months. Gloria Bush, 72, who was also homeless due to severe mental illness, died of complications from hypothermia in December.

* * *

How in the world could this happen to someone? Thirty-four years? That is impossible!

The problem of California's homelessness epidemic was often in the news, but it was far across the country, out of my realm of life, falling into a category of "other peoples' problems." When we watched stories on the news about California's homeless problems, we thought that certainly there were many experts in that field who could and should fix the situation. In my life, I did not know anyone who was ever close to being homeless.

Where would I even start with all this new information? I had to start again with grieving. Mom used to say, "Tears wash the heart," and they did. This latest development landed squarely on my heart, but it also had to sink into my brain, the whole tragedy of it. It did not seem real. It could not be real.

CHAPTER THIRTY-SEVEN

At the very least, my starting point was in getting a copy of a death certificate for Bunny. From that form I learned her true date of birth and could then send away for a birth certificate.

She was actually thirteen years older than me. I tried to picture having an older sister like that, but it was inconceivable, not because of her living status, but only because I could not imagine the reality of having any siblings. I was trying to stay in the real world to comprehend all of it.

Bunny had died of septic shock, pneumonia, and anemia. She also suffered from rheumatoid arthritis. Since she apparently died in the hospital, I was grateful that she was in a comfortable bed, indoors, and hopefully, not alone. I could not help but picture her life as lonely, neglected, and unloved at the time but that was only my imagination working overtime.

Most of the other blanks on her death certificate were completed as "UNKNOWN." Her body was unclaimed and cremated by a local funeral service and the "Place of Final Disposition" was "Scattered at sea off the coast of San Francisco County." The article had said that Palo Alto was her "home." For me, it was another "relative" tossed into the Pacific Ocean.

I read the article about Bunny over again. There were several people quoted and mentioned. Maybe I could talk to them? Certainly, the author of the article might remember writing the story and may have even known her personally. I looked up the *Palo Alto Weekly*, called the number, and got an answering machine for Ms. Dremann, delighted that she still worked there.

Finally, I was able to speak with her. It was very kind of her to call me back, but I was disappointed that she was not able to provide more details, saying that everything she knew was in her article. But that was a start and I thanked her for her article and for speaking with me. I wanted her to understand that if she had not written that story, I doubt seriously if I would have ever found Bunny at all. I decided to go down the names in the story, hungry for anything someone could reveal.

The second paragraph listed the All Saints Episcopal Church where a memorial service was held for her. I was an Episcopalian at the time and was delighted at the possibility that my church had done such a nice honor for her, hoping that perhaps, Bunny might have been a member or affiliated with the church in some way, even if not a regular attendee. That would certainly be yet another coincidence, sharing the same church affiliation.

I spoke with the church secretary, explaining my unusual situation. She said Bunny was not listed as a member, but that she would leave a message for the priest. He had been there several years, and I was optimistic he may have known her very well, perhaps my best hope. He was on leave and would be back in a few weeks.

Over the next six months, I never heard from the priest. I left about five messages, including on his personal voicemail. He never called and would not take my call. He could have said to me that he did not know her, but he never did even that. One piece of information that the secretary revealed was that the memorial service was organized by a woman named Faith Bell. She owned a well-known, very popular bookstore called Bell's Books, in Palo Alto.

I think I could have talked to Faith Bell for hours. She had really liked Bunny, in spite of her difficult lifestyle circumstances. She described Bunny as fearless but extremely calm in her demeanor. She did not want anyone to control her. She was very clearly making all her own choices. Bunny was extremely interested in local politics and attended most Palo Alto city council meetings and hearings, speaking often on the record.

Faith Bell recalled that in Bunny's last days, she was seen sleeping in a doorway behind the bank. A local lady brought her food and performed some degree of hospice for her. Faith organized the memorial service for Bunny as a remembrance. It was held in the church nursery and was not officiated by anyone at the church.

Faith told me that "everybody loved Bunny" but only about twenty people attended. Faith provided some flowers. The one question that Faith could not answer was how she had become homeless and remained that way for thirty-four years. She did not know. I thanked her for her kindness to Bunny and now to me too, and additionally for creating the memorial service.

The next easily findable contact in the article would be Police Chief Dennis Burns. He had been a police officer since 1982 and he remembered Bunny very fondly. He told me she was a lovely person, a description I did not expect to hear from someone she had likely perturbed by her lifestyle alone. He described her as an independent and kind soul and then he said she was a sweet soul. It was his understanding that she had had a high position in the tech industry in her past and he found her to be actually brilliant.

Chief Burns said that in spite of Bunny's living arrangements, she was never any trouble at all. She did not drink alcohol or do drugs, and for whatever reason, Bunny was happy with her lifestyle. He and other officers used to give her coffee, especially in cold weather. He had no idea how she ended up homeless.

Somewhere between Maggie's death in 1969 and 1980, something had happened to Bunny. Her place of living, the address listed on the death certificate, had been with her grandmother Maggie on Cowper Street. Perhaps she took care of Maggie in her last years. As yet, no one could tell me what happened between those years.

Chief Burns confirmed that towards the end of her life, Bunny had an opportunity to go to Lytton Gardens, a subsidized type of housing, but then she chose not to go there. I thanked him for taking such good care of her through the years. I told him that, in my opinion, trying to protect the homeless must be a real challenge for all police officers. Most officers are such dedicated individuals who rarely get credit for their difficult work. He remarked again that Bunny was never a problem.

CHAPTER THIRTY-EIGHT

Throughout all my phone calls to people in California, I continually relayed my newfound information to my longtime childhood friend, Thelma. We had been friends since I was eight years old. She was excited at every new bit of news.

At one point in the revelations of Bunny's past, she asked me, "How does it feel to find all this stuff out?" Without much hesitation, I answered that for the most part, it felt like I had somehow always known her and now I was just filling in some missing pieces.

It was time to delve into the technical side, the medical explanation for all this, so I tracked down the Dr. Joel Wolfberg quoted in the article. He had volunteered his time with the Santa Clara County Behavioral Health Services Department, in a program called Momentum for Mental Health.

Dreading to encounter stuffy professionalism due to his title, I was delightfully relieved to find that he was quite the opposite, and he started off asking me to call him Joel. His warm, friendly manner immediately put my heart at ease. He was extremely knowledgeable about Bunny and very fond of her up until her death.

Joel shared that Bunny was eccentric. Considering her last thirty-four years, that almost seemed like an understatement, especially if she had actually maintained that lifestyle by her own choice. He said that at times, she could definitely be cantankerous. *Cantankerous? A relative of moi?* I could just hear my dad telling me I was hopelessly impertinent when I was young, his exact words.

Medically speaking, Joel diagnosed her as paranoid schizophrenic and said it was really a shame because she never took treatment for it. He did not offer an explanation for why she refused treatment, and I did not pressure him to do so. I wondered if that had anything to do with the "cantankerous" adjective.

In my imagination, I pictured a dedicated doctor volunteering his time to help many people and Bunny simply refusing the help. My own memory recalled several times when I argued with my doctors and resisted their recommended treatment. (Eventually losing my gall bladder, for example, I had to eat crow that time and admit he had been right all along.)

Joel also knew her well enough to share some background information about Bunny. She not only had a math degree from the University of Chicago but a master's degree from Stanford. *Math? You must be kidding,* I thought to myself.

During high school, when I applied at Northwestern University to satisfy my parents' hopes, I aspired to study journalism. Notably, Northwestern had a reputation as the best journalism school in the country. I had to submit an example of my writing ability. They were very kind in their rejection letter and softened the blow with an offer of a free year of math study. Math had always been my strong suit. It was so easy that it was terribly boring no matter what level I tried.

Joel said Bunny was nearly obsessed with rabbits, hence the nickname. At that point, I did not confess my affection for them to the good doctor! In spite of being homeless, Bunny had two live rabbits as pets. After one of them died, she applied to the rabbit rescue society, but they would not give her another because she was homeless.

Indeed, her love of rabbits was one of the things that made her so well liked in her community. Under the online version of the Palo Alto article, I was able to read numerous posted comments that referred to Bunny's rabbits as well as her extremely independent personality.

In the online comments, most people wished her the traditional affection of "Rest in peace, Bunny." One lady recalled a story that Bunny had asked if her family could help store some of her belongings in their storage shed in their backyard. She paid them $20 a month and they called it "Bunny money."

CHAPTER THIRTY-NINE

Thanks to the information in the article, my last contact person in California would prove to be the most valuable to my heart. Of all the people I spoke with who seemed to "love" her, this man obviously cared for Bunny the most.

Heiri Schupisser was a specialist in homeless outreach at the same nonprofit Momentum for Mental Health where I had found Joel. When we began to talk, Heiri had recently retired. He had a picture of her on his home workshop wall as a remembrance. He called her an "angel without wings."

While he told me the stories, he painted the picture of a woman who was very stubborn and principled. He did not know a lot about her personal past except that she used to tell him that her ex-husband "got us to the moon." According to her, he worked in the science of rocket fuel.

Bunny was a great writer, according to Heiri, and was very interested in politics, writing many, many letters to anyone and everyone, and often to California Senator, Dianne Feinstein. He could not tell me if Bunny was a fan or a critic, or particularly Republican or Democrat, just passionate about her beliefs. She was extremely interested in all aspects of her community and was a regular attendee at the monthly city council meetings, addressing her concerns in comments when it was her turn at the podium.

In spite of her difficult life on the streets, she never panhandled or begged. People would often give her things and the local police officers would give her coffee and food. She had been raped at least once, probably by gang members. She had been beaten up and lost one eye, after which she often walked with her head lowered.

Heiri tried for years to get Bunny into assisted living, but she was adamant that she would only go to Lytton Gardens—for some unknown reason. When an opening finally occurred, she chose not to accept.

Bunny lived off her Social Security and perhaps some welfare payments. She never spent her money on cigarettes, alcohol, or drugs. She had a bank account. She even had a will. In her will, she left all her money to the Rabbit Rescue Society in San Francisco. Among her personal belongings in a storage container, she had $66,000 in cash when she passed away.

Heiri sent me the following picture he had on his wall. It would be the only certain picture of her I would acquire. Thankfully, the "angel without wings" was smiling.

About two nights after I received her picture from Heiri, I had a dream. It was very short, but I can still remember it vividly, unlike many dreams. My husband and I were in a quiet restaurant somewhere, sitting at a small round table with high-seated chairs, the kind your legs can dangle from. There were very few people in the restaurant, as if they weren't really open for business or were just in between busy times.

Bunny came into the restaurant and walked up to our table as if we were supposed to meet her there, definitely meeting each other for the first time. She was dressed exactly like the picture except that she had no hat. She did not have any odor, but I could tell she was not really very clean. We looked at each other and hugged. I can still feel that hug as if it really happened. She sat down with us at the table and the dream ended.

CHAPTER FORTY

Perhaps because Bunny had lived on the streets for such a long time, even Joel and Heiri could not tell me exactly how she ended up there. I was beginning to believe that only Bunny knew the answer to that question.

Joel had mentioned that she had a "boyfriend" at the University of Chicago and that she used to tell everyone that her ex-husband "got us to the moon." There was a slight chance that perhaps her boyfriend may have become more than a boyfriend. Somebody had to be the "Good" part to form her last name since she was actually born Valerie Ryan.

At about the same time, I was researching other cousins on Ancestry. One cousin told me they had found information about Bunny's education at the University of Chicago and of her husband's, also. He sent me their graduation programs.

Bunny had graduated with a Bachelor of Science in mathematics. Someone with the last name of Good graduated with a master's in physics. Coincidence? I searched his name and unfortunately found his fairly recent obituary. He had passed away in 2011 but it listed a wife and three children. It would be another long shot.

I found an address for one name, a daughter, and sat down to write a letter of basically, outright shameless begging. I explained what I was trying to do, to find some information on Bunny, hoping I had the right person. I tried to be clear that I was not a nut, which sounds ridiculous, but in this day and time, it seemed appropriate to at least try to allay her fears.

I mailed the letter Certified, Restricted Delivery so that it could only be delivered to that exact person with proof of identification required. It would protect both of our private interests to prevent the letter from ending up in anyone's hands. I saw it was scanned "Delivered" and she was brave enough to call me soon after. I'll call her Debbie. We were not physically related because Bunny had no children with Debbie's father. They were indeed married for a short time.

Debbie was delightful to speak with and could not have been more gracious. She shared many stories that she remembered from growing up; the family called them "Bunny stories." One of them explained how they became aware of Bunny many years ago. It went something like this:

Somewhere around the early 1980s, Bunny was apparently living in her car in front of a business in Palo Alto. The business complained to the police and an officer picked her up for vagrancy. Years ago, it was against the law to live on the street or be homeless.

At the police station, the police officer explained to Bunny that she could not live in her car as she had been doing and that she needed to make another plan. Was there someone she could call to come get her? She answered that the only person she knew was her ex-husband and he was a physicist, and she did not want to bother him.

The officer gave her these choices, "Ok ma'am, I may not be a "rocket scientist" myself but the way I see this situation is that *physically* you can't be living in your car like that so you have to be *physically* somewhere else. As I recall, I think that was one of the laws of physics back in my high school science class. So, here are your other "somewhere else" choices: you can either go into drug rehab, but I don't think you need that, or you can go to a motel if you have the money for a room, or you can call a relative to come get you, or we can put you in jail. You pick."

Bunny agreed to call her ex-husband and he came down and got her out of jail. From that point on, they used to see each other occasionally for lunch as friends. He would try to help her out sometimes. Indeed, for many years, he and his wife generously tried to help Bunny financially. On one occasion, he offered to give her money to get her teeth fixed. She responded that if he wanted to give her money, fine, but not to tell her how to spend it.

In Debbie's father's obituary, a description of him had read: He (her father) was fiercely independent and he passionately believed in everyone's right to live exactly as they pleased. I have to wonder if that statement might have referred to Bunny.

From all appearances, it seems safe to say that Bunny indeed lived life the way she wanted. Personally, I do not understand why she wanted to live like she did. I'm not sure I could understand it even if she were here to explain it to me.

I love my home and we have made many sacrifices to make it a safe and comfortable refuge from the worldly elements—such as difficult weather and crime. Our choices through all the years prioritized enjoying life but planning for the inevitable rainy day when our life's direction and resources could change dramatically. We are not wealthy, but we try to be prepared.

When Dad had asked Mrs. Walrath at The Cradle "What will she be like?" she answered him, "She will be like you," reassuringly. But of course, realistically, who can know? The old question of nature versus nurture will always be with us. Indeed, that had been one of the fundamental basics of Dad's college degree in psychology, studying that same question.

As individual people, are we what we learn from others, or are we pre-coded to be a certain way? As soon as that question is answered in one way, it will prove a falsehood the day after because another person's life story will prove the opposite. Are we influenced by our teachings and childhood? Certainly. Do we see amazing similarities in the actions and mannerisms of our family members? Certainly. Are we predestined to have a specific path or are we totally in the driver's seat?

Perhaps the only thing that we really know is that God gave his children free will to make our own choices, evaluate our options, observe the world we live in, learn from our past, and choose our steps going forward every day, every moment. Ideally, we learn as we go, through our own mistakes and triumphs, and watching other people's trials and successes through a broad study of history.

Of course, every decision we make, every choice has a consequence, too. Those consequences we experience are the "feedback" we get telling us our choice was right or wrong. This is not to say that some people don't have insurmountable physical or mental problems and must depend on others. There will always be those who desperately rely on our compassion as humans because they are incapable of taking care of themselves. But for the rest of us, our choices are all ours. So are our consequences.

As long as Bunny was not infringing on someone else's rights or someone else's property, she was just as free to make her choices as all of us. It appears that she only stayed on private property, and apparently with the permission of that property owner. She did not impede public areas or block access to public sidewalks and places. She acted respectfully toward the rest of her community and took an interest in its well-being. She did not require others to take care of her or provide her sustenance. She obeyed laws. She never begged.

As far as I could tell, she never blamed others for her situation, nor demanded that someone else help her. Indeed, she chose quite the opposite, to *not* have people help her and to keep herself free. Perhaps she suffered from mental illness but even that involved a choice which she freely made, to not receive "treatment" for whatever reasons. According to the experts, she supposedly suffered from depression but who in this world has not? She was pragmatic, capable, analytical, and sober. She made her choices clearly based on her own principles and preferences.

By all accounts, Bunny appears to have been fearless. As a remarkable testament to her extraordinary reservoir of courage, she did not appear to let fear rule her choices. She and I may have shared many attributes through some mysterious pattern woven by our Maker, but I do not think I could have accomplished what she did with her grace and that smile. I wholeheartedly admire her own immense heart and strength and especially, her bravery.

Rest in peace, Bunny.

EPILOGUE

This search has been quite a journey, finding happiness and sadness in all the pages, just like in every life. I am so grateful for the people who helped me along the way. Many offered strong support, the kind you can really feel. Many generously gave good ideas, information, advice, and a lot of listening time. Even beyond listening, it is so very valuable to hear each other and respond. Even Bunny did not live in a vacuum. We need to respond to each other.

I have been so very blessed, by my family, my country, my small world of life, and my God. My birth parents gave me the greatest gift they could at the time, life itself. My adoptive parents gave me the next greatest gifts: their love and their time. I pray that my readers will be blessed also and see the great good we all have in our world if we just search for it.

This book is all about the choices we make in life. I have also tried to portray historically the choices I have witnessed in our culture. We may all have some things in our life we cannot control. Aside from that, our choices are our choices. Some days, appreciating our world can be a good choice just for starters, and we can choose upwards from there. Bunny made the most of her world and apparently never seemed to feel sorry for what she did not have, except maybe for one more rabbit.

My search actually does not end with this story. During the writing of this book, another half-sister, Marjorie (her actual name), whom I had never heard of or knew existed, popped up on the very top of my DNA list of relatives. I sent her a message, but she has yet to answer my note. Maybe tomorrow.

This passage was handwritten by my Mom inside the front cover of my baby book. My apologies; there was no author listed on the original page, but the author might forgive us. It read as follows:

The Answer (To An Adopted Child)

Not flesh of my flesh,
Nor bone of my bone
But still miraculously
    my own
Never forget
for a single minute,
you didn't grow under
my heart,
But in it.
    Mother

For as many as are led by the Spirit of God,
they are the sons of God.

For ye have not received the spirit of bondage again to fear;
but ye have received the Spirit of adoption,
whereby we cry, Father.

The Spirit itself beareth witness with our spirit,
that we are the children of God:

And, if children, then heirs;
heirs of God, and joint-heirs with Christ;
if so be that we suffer with him,
that we may be also glorified together.
Romans 8: 14-17

ABOUT THE AUTHOR

Susan D. Guillotte has worked as a waitress, a bank teller, an accountant, a bed & breakfast owner, and a postal clerk, and she has always wanted to be a writer. Someone once told her to "write what you know," so she did, and here it is. Susan lives with her husband, Newfoundland dogs, and their one-eyed $3,000 "$5-cat" in Eastern Virginia.

She may be contacted at BunnybySusanDGuillotte@gmail.com

www.ingramcontent.com/pod-product-compliance
Lightning Source LLC
Chambersburg PA
CBHW060232030426
42335CB00014B/1420